"...Peter, spread the words, spread the messages far and wide for they are powerful, they are important, they have been on the shelf in My Heart and now is the time that this book is to be open and the Wisdom and Knowledge of My and My Father's Will and My and My Mother's Heart be shared, be digested by all My children so that the Kingdom can be established here on this Earth as it is in Heaven. Peter, I mean this, I want this done, this is My Will, this is My Directive to you and all that are helping you. Now, My son, now, be Apostles of the Last Days, the last days of this Era and the first days of the new Era, the Era of the Divine Will. Peter, be a total and complete nobody and I mean a nothing. Have absolutely no will of your own in any way so that I can reign and I will reign. You will be My Flower in the garden, you will be an Apostle of My Love of My Sacred Heart, of My Mother's Heart. Peter, I am serious, this is Jesus your Lord talking to you and you are My Special Instrument..." April 29, 1994 PM 11:00

"...Peter, you are my special child. You must love others unconditionally, you must love others with my Heart, with my Son's Heart. You must love them divinely. This is your calling, one of love. Share His Love, spread His Love, for Love will triumph, it will win. This is God's Will for the Earth. God the Father created all and He can make any changes He desires to and He loves His Creatures and is going to make the changes necessary in order that His Will will reign in all hearts, in all lives, in all of creation, for when men's hearts are changed then all will be in harmony..." May 10, 1994 PM 07:45

"...My dear child, this is your Mother, I love you, Jesus is my Lord and Savior! Thank you for your work on the next book. You must get this second book out as quickly as possible also for my children must have hope in the future
PM 02:00

HIS KINGDOM COME

HIS WILL BE DONE

DEDICATION

To the Edification, Exhortation and Comfort

of

the Church, the Body of Christ

Re: 1st Corinthians, Chapter 14

"Not everyone that saith to me 'Lord, Lord' shall enter into the Kingdom of Heaven; but he that doth the Will of My Father who is in Heaven, he shall enter into the Kingdom of Heaven" Matthew (7:21)

Table of Contents

APRIL, 1994 13

MAY, 1994 75

Appendix 135

Index 139

Concordance 147

FOREWORD

At the end of December, 1993, Peter recited a nine day Novena to the Holy Spirit, not realizing that on the day the Novena ended, he was to attend a retreat service given by a well known Catholic Priest, Father McCarthy. The next morning Jesus spoke to his heart during Communion. That afternoon, he went to confession with Father McCarthy and was told by Jesus through Father to begin writing down what would come to him after prayer (quiet time) each day. He followed these instructions by the Priest and the result is the "Triumph of Love" and this book. A few weeks after he started writing down these words, Peter received an unsolicited phone call from a locutionist, Ken Hipps, that confirmed that Jesus was speaking to his heart. The message from Ken Hipps is found in the appendix. Peter is a cradle Catholic with five brothers and sisters. He is an engineer and has been married for sixteen years. Peter is formally consecrated as a slave to Jesus per the St. Louis Marie De Montfort method. He is also formally consecrated to the Divine Will per "The Community of the Sons of the Divine Will" in St. Cloud, Florida. Peter has been very active in starting a new business over the last three years. This endeavor has resulted in much humiliation and hardship, physically, mentally and financially. He is quite involved in local Civic and Church organizations. The messages promise great hope for the future, the new Era. He was told to distribute the messages and that they would help others as they have helped him. He has also begun regular visits to a Catholic Priest who has agreed to be his spiritual director. Peter continues to receive messages at the time of publication.

These teachings and lessons on the Divine Will are not as detailed or as extensive as those given in the thirty six volumes written by Luisa Piccarreta over a period of thirty nine years (Luisa died March 4, 1947) and distributed by the Catholic Priests of the "Community of the Sons of the Divine Will", P.O. Box 701327, St. Cloud, FL 34770-1327, Telephone: 407-957-3850. Peter believes that the messages were given to help him and his brothers and sisters in Christ to more easily grasp this new gift from the Father and aid in understanding the Divine Will teachings given to Luisa, the Father's Plan for the future; "Thy Will be done on Earth as it is in Heaven" Matthew (6:10)(see the 'Introduction' to this book). This book is a sequel to the "Triumph of Love". The "Triumph of Love" contains important lessons about the Divine Will, including how to live in peace, the necessity of having great trust in the Father's Love, the importance of humility, giving up of the human will - being a nothing, detachment from creatures and the world, and our membership in the Family of God.

These words dictated to Peter are presented in the order they were received, however, to fully comprehend these messages, it is important to understand the differences and relationships between 'having the Will of God' which is a Gift from the Father, 'living in the Will of God' which is a way or state of life and 'doing the Will of God' which is the active life of a Christian. The majority of the messages can be placed into one of these three categories. The message that best explains this relationship between having, living and doing the Divine Will is that of April 11, 1994, @ 2:30 PM. Additionally, the message of May 1, 1994 @ 3:00 AM is an excellent summary of the concrete way to live in the Divine Will while still on Earth.

The messages teach that we are in a state of spiritual childhood and that this state of spiritual childhood, not being childish, but being childlike, is pleasing to our Heavenly Family. It is important to realize that from a spiritual standpoint we are just infants in our knowledge and especially knowledge of this new gift of the Divine Will. It is very 'biblical' to be a child in our relationship with our Divine Family. In the previous book the messages indicated that the Blessed Virgin Mary desired this intimacy. For example, Mary said that she preferred to be called 'Mommy' or 'Mom' instead of 'Mother'. Likewise, the words 'Daddy' and 'Brother' are used at times, apparently to show the intimacy desired by God the Father and Jesus Christ our Savior.

INTRODUCTION

(Announcement of a new Gift of God)

"My son, life in the Will is awesome, it is great, it gets better as you get in the groove, for the Divine Will is the best of the best. So, My son, as you said today, announce that We are on the threshold of the new Era and the Father has a new and wonderful Gift for His Children and yes, My son, it is analogous to the announcement of the Gift of the Holy Spirit made by the Apostles and Disciples. Peter, don't hold back, stay in the forefront, you have My Spirit and now you have My Will and all My Children of My Heart are entitled to this Gift for it is a Divine Gift, a Gift from God the Father and now is the time for My Children to receive this Gift. Peter, without a doubt, this Gift is great for it is meant to bring in the Reign of the Father's Will in all souls, the Prayer of the Son answered and now with the Reign of the two Hearts, the Heart of Sacred Love and the Heart of Sinless, Immaculate Purity, the creature will be a new creation, made anew, reborn into the image of the Son and now all will be true Sons and Daughters of Love, Divine Love and Sons and Daughters of the Divine Will! Now is the time, now is the beginning for all to hear, all to receive, all to be transformed into Children of God! So, Peter, the fullness of *redemption is on the horizon and the treasure at the end of the rainbow awaits all creatures that accept the truth! Love the truth, open their hearts, open to be filled, to be united to Our Hearts and give up completely their will and receive the Divine Will of the Father and this renewal together with the rebirth of the creature with the Spirit of God completes the Father's Plan to return the creature to the original design for the creature before the Fall. This long awaited return is beginning to occur in your midst and now this good news of the Kingdom coming needs to be announced with great fervor, with great love, with great anticipation of a full saturation of the entire world hearing this good news and receiving the Father's Will into their soul and living and doing His Will each moment for the rest of eternity! Rejoice! My son, be in wonderment, live on the wave, the tidal wave of My Love which will cover the Earth! I love you Peter, My Son of My Will, peace be with you."*

"I love You, my King and Savior." June 3, 1994 PM 10:35

"...YOU WILL NOT DIE BUT LIVE ETERNALLY" April 3, 1994 AM 06:00

"I have risen, I have truly risen. I have conquered death, conquered evil, conquered the world. Sin has no power. My son, the Easter Message is one of great hope. There will be no death. Keep this truth in front of you and meditate on it often. My son, you have a busy day today. Please stay in My Peace. Please let Me shine. The mission has been planned. I need to use you. My son, contemplate just how much I love you. Have a beautiful day without a care or concern of the future, for I am in control of the future and you will not die but live eternally. I love you, My son. Deliver My Peace, My Joy, My Love to all those I place you with. Go now, enveloped in a cloud of pure love."

"I love You, my Lord, my God."

"...DON'T BE A SLAVE TO MATERIAL WANTS AND DESIRES" April 3, 1994 PM 11:45

"My son, happy are those that do My Will with joy, with peace, with contentment, for they live in My Will. They are My Sons and Daughters of My Will. My son, how many think they are living in My Will but are still in their maze, the maze of their own will, for they won't let go of their wants and desires. They are living among the gravestones in the cemetery of the dying world. How long do they think they can hang on to the world? Will they follow their material desires to Hell?, for they must get off the band wagon and free themselves of this slavery of their lusts for material goods or it will pull them down, down, down to the netherworld. No gods before Me, no idols. I speak not of golden calves but I speak of anything that interferes with their walk with Me, with their striving to do My Will. My son, do you think that all the possessions that My Children have bring them closer to Me? No, they do not, they only divert their attention and time away from their God. My

Children, rid yourself of unnecessary goods and material possessions. Live simply. When I lived with My Mother and Father, Mary and Joseph, we lived very simply in order to show an example of not being all wrapped up in the goods of the world. My son, these material possessions are the result of a pride and ego that rules in My Children. They must have, they must own. They must have more than others, they must be secure, they must have pleasures and comforts. All of this only serves to divert the creature's attention from their God. I am not saying that all must live a life of poverty, no, I am saying don't be a slave to material wants and desires. You should only own what you need, what is necessary to practice your vocation and raise a family. If it is unnecessary, then it interferes with our relationship, with doing My Will, for I did not create you or any of My Creatures to spend all their time using or fixing or shopping for material possessions. I, the Lord, say; Enough is enough. Rid your house of all the junk, the extra stuff, the clutter of the world and spend your time on Me, on learning about Me, on praying to Me, on serving Me by helping others and loving others, by spreading the good news of the Gospel. My Children, you have been deceived by the evil one, you have fallen prey to his temptations, you have taken hook, line and sinker. My Children, I love you, I want you all to myself. I am jealous of time wasted. Please, My Children, change your ways now. Be My Children of simplicity, of poverty of spirit, of peace by living in the world but out of this world. Have no anchors, this is not your homeland, Heaven is. Cast away from the shoreline of the city of wants and needs and sail onto the ocean of love, an ocean of living and practicing love of God and love of neighbor, an ocean where you walk on the water by total trust in the love that God has for you and thereby know that God will supply all your needs, an ocean where the line of sight is clear and you can determine direction and fly as the crow flies, directly into My Arms, into My Love, without having to stumble and fall over useless things. My Children, please, once and for all pull out of it, break away, pull the rip cord, jump ship, live in My Will and do My Will and My Will is that you live by My

Example, live the life that I lived when I lived in My Earthly Life. Peter, do you understand that life is passing and soon the world will be changing? This is especially not the time to be wrapped up in materialism, for you and all My Children need to concentrate on preparing for My Coming and living through the storm, which can only be accomplished by practicing and developing a very close relationship with Me and by praying and trusting. My son, as I have said before, the time to prepare is now, so live a life of abandonment and surrender, live as I have been teaching you, live only for love. Be My Soldier of Love and depend on Me for everything now and during the storm and thereafter. Peter, I am sorry to be so harsh with My Words, I am trying to wake you up and wake up all those that will read these words. I do it because I love you and the others and I don't want you or them trapped in this rut of materialism. Peace, My son, Love, My son, Joy, My son. I am with you, I am in you, I love you, I hold you in My Arms and protect you with My Love, goodnight."

"I love You, my King, my Lord, my Savior."

"...REFLECT THE LIGHT OF THE 'SON'" April 4, 1994 AM 06:45

"My son, another day has started, another day to love. My son, live without care of the future, live only for today, reflect the light of the 'Son'. Be Me to all. Peace, My son, I love you. Go now, start the day, I am with you."

"I love You, my King."

"BE REALISTIC AND FUTURE MINDED" April 4, 1994 PM 01:00

"My son, happy are those that live in My Will, for they desire only what God wants and God plans for their life. They have no desires or ambitions for worldly fame or material wealth. They have no desire to climb to the top of the corporate ladder. They only desire to please the Father. This is the simple Gospel Truth, to decrease so that God increases.

15

My son, how can one live in the world and not become attached, not become all wrapped up in the flesh, in becoming the best in their career? Well, one must have a different perspective than those that live in the world. They must be realistic and future minded. How can anyone not be aware that all creatures have a limited life span on this Earth? and no one, no human being has ever conquered death, only I have conquered death and rose from the dead, so all is passing, all is temporary, all is a facade, all is without any real long term purpose except preparing for your rising to new life in Eternity. My son, I proved that, by following Me, My Children can live eternally. No others have offered this reality, so live to please Me which is the same as living to please the Father and to please the Father He wants you to do what He says, act the way He wants you to act, live a life united to Him, in short, doing His Will, the Divine Will. Peter, to strive to please the Father by striving to determine and do His Will is the ultimate goal of yourself and all of My Family of Christians and all of mankind, but they have been blinded so I must shake them up in a big way and hence the trial. My son, all must choose, they must either begin to live to please Me and do God's Will or they will perish. So, My son, if you and the others begin to live in the Will of God and do the Will of God each day of your life, then you will please God and usher in the new Era of Love, of Divine Will, for His Will will rule and all will be done in accordance to His Designs. So, My son, be future oriented, be My son that serves others and lives in and does My Will. I love you Peter. My Will for you is to live as I have been teaching you. Review and study My Words and make them a part of your being. Go now into the world again, but live in My Will."

"I love You, my King."

"...BE UNITED TO GOD'S WILL!" April 4, 1994 PM 11:00
"My son, how blessed are those who strive to live in and do the Will of the Father! It is only by doing His Will that

you can experience an unending love for others, an unending love for the Trinity. My son, how many times must the creature fall and stumble before learning that his human will is chaos, is confusion, is endless wandering without direction, without purpose, without peace? My son, to live in the Will of God is order, is wisdom, is peace, for God is the First and the Last, God is the Creator, God is the Almighty, God is in control of all activities, all creatures, all spirits, all of Creation and to live in God's Will is to be united to the mind of the Creator, to be one with God, is to be in harmony with all of Creation, to be a son or daughter that does not contradict God's Will but is united to It with a union that is at peace with the Fiat of the Father, the Fiat of the Son, the Fiat of the Holy Spirit, the Fiat of the Blessed Virgin. Oh, My Son of My Father's Will, be united to your God in body, soul and spirit. Live and act in one accord with His Directives, His Word, His Love, His Care for you. My son, Oh what a gift is yours to be united to God's Will! It is a gift that is above all other graces that can be given to the creature, a gift that cannot be taken lightly, for to be united with God's Will is to have no will of your own, is to be as a tree in a forest, serene and calm, strong and stable, even with gusty winds. It is to be an unmovable rock on the shoreline of an ocean beach where the waves pound and thrash and clamor but no movement occurs. The rock knows no fear, no anxiety, no unrest. It takes the beating of the waves and is unaffected by the storm. My son, you are not a rock, you are a creature with your own human will, with the capability of deciding for yourself, but you must sacrifice your will totally and take on and replace your will with God's Will, with God's Wants and Desires, with God's Demands and Needs. So, My son, kill your will, strangle your desires, cut off your thoughts of the past and future. Live in the present moment, live in peace even in the midst of storm winds and crashing seas. Be stable as a rock on the sea shore, anchored in the Will of God, the Creator of the Universe. My son, God is Love defined. He has only one desire and need from His Creatures, an unending thirst for love from His Sons and Daughters, for He is a Father, He is the Father, He is a perfect Father. He only needs love from His Children, He only cares to be loved and treated as an Earthly Father desires when He comes home from work and is greeted by all his children with hugs and kisses and has to stop everything to listen to how the little one, his smallest child, did at his first day of school. My son, treat the Father as you would treat your Earthly Father if you were a small innocent child. Be little, be loving, be trusting, be dependent, be the favorite son of his, the one that always wants to please his Father by what he says or does or how he treats others. My son, be proud of your Father and stand up for Him if others speak ill of Him. My son, be a son that comes to his Father for every need and discusses his problems for God the Father is a Father of love. Don't fear your Dad, love Him! My son, My brother. I love you and I will help you to love the Father with My Love, with My Heart. Peter, you are one with the Father's Will when you are without a will, when you are truly a nothing, an empty vessel, a being that invites the Father's Will, the Son's Love and the Holy Spirit's Peace into your being. You are a reflection of God the Father when you are possessed by His Holy Will. My son, be a volcano filled with the heat of God's Love, a love that even melts a mountain of stone, a volcano that shoots forth great light of the fire of love, a volcano that is being controlled by God the Father's Will. My son, you are united to God because your love is united to His and He dwells inside you, so be always striving to live in and do the right, the just, the perfect Will of God. Rest now, My son, sleep in the Arms of your Father in front of the fireplace in a mountain cabin with your head resting on His Heart and His Eyes and Smile saying 'I love you, My son'."

"I love You, goodnight my Jesus, thank You for Your Words."

"You're welcome, peace be with you, rest now Peter."

"...LIVE IN HIS WILL AND HAVE PEACE, LOVE, JOY" April 5, 1994 AM 06:10

"My son, to live in My Will is to know that all your Earthly needs, all your problems, all your cares and plans are and will be taken care of because God is omnipotent and God is in control of even the tiniest insect. My son, live in His Will and have peace, love, joy. Stop treading water and let God's Will support you. Care not of worldly matters, they are passing. Do what is important for the moment and live in His Will, His Love, His Care, His Peace. My son, if you were a child again and you lived at home and your Earthly Father supported you, would you be concerned about anything? Well, My son, this is how it is now. Your Heavenly Father is providing all your needs so live and do His Will and He will care for and protect you and His Peace will reign, His Love will reign in your being. Each hour ask to be inspired by the Holy Spirit who permanently lives inside your being to know and do what is God's Will in the current circumstances of your Earthly life. He will guide you and inspire you. My son, trust in My Love for you and as I have been teaching you, know that in God's Will Love reigns and without doubt, without worry, know that everything is under control. So, My son, walk on the water trusting that God's Will will support you and guide you and uplift you to a plane out of the maze of the world to a plane that is Heaven on Earth, a plane where you can be clear headed and at peace, so My Love can be exploding out of you to all you meet and are with each day of your life. Go now and start the day. The mission has been finalized. You have your orders, love, love, love!"

"I love You, my Lord and Savior."

"...THE PLANE OF THE DIVINE WILL..." April 5, 1994 PM 01:30

"My son, to live in My Divine Will is peace without end, is joy without measure, is love beyond comprehension. To live in My Will is to be one with the Will of the Trinity. Just

as a team of football players all execute a play together because they all have the knowledge of the play, so it is with those that are members of My Body that live in My Will. A team player must listen to the quarterback and do his part in the play. He can not do what he thinks is best or what he wants to do, he must do the will of the quarterback. If all team members do the will of the quarterback, the play will be successful and the team will win. The same is true for soldiers in a battle. They must follow the will of the General, they must be in union with the commander or the soldiers may be hurt or killed. So, My son, My Body must do the Will of the Father or they will slip and fall and be carried away to Hell. My son, to live in and do the Father's Will is the reasonable, practical, prudent decision to make, for the Father only wants what is best for each of His Children and within His Will is order and peace and love. My Body, My Team must unite under one commander and live in and follow all the directions from above, for Divine Wisdom is undeniable, it is truth, it is pure goodness. So, My son, live in His Will, His Plan for you, His Providence, His Care. Peter, all that is necessary is the desire to live detached completely from the world and detached from creatures and detached from thoughts that hinder His Will. To be in the plane of the Divine Will it is necessary to live moment by moment in a trusting, abandoned and surrendered state. My son, God's Plan for you is in His Will. It is written in His Heart. Only concern yourself with living in His Will and following His Directions given in His Gospel and by the Church, the true Church. My son, I love you unfathomably and am caring for you. Back into the world, back to the mission, back to the certainty of and security of living in the Father's Will."

"I love You, my King."

"...TAKE TIME OUT OF YOUR READING AND SLEEP TIME TO PRAY..." April 5, 1994 PM 10:15
"My son, won't you please take the time to pray for the

salvation of souls? Time is short, justice will strike and lives will be lost. So, My son, pray for souls. Peter, please take time out of your reading and sleep time to pray for souls! Thank you, My son, in advance. My son, tomorrow's mission is all planned. Be sure to concentrate on loving them, not on worldly matters. Rest now, My son, in My Arms."

"I love You, my Jesus."

"...STRIVE FOR THE FINISH LINE OF HOLINESS..."
April 6, 1994 AM 05:30

"My son, happy are those that dwell in the Heart of their King, their lives are only love, their joy is serving the Lord, their peace is residing in the Arms of the Father's Bosom! My son, happy are those who seek perfection in their lives, they walk with the Angels, they maintain a serene and calm manner, they are guided by the Holy Spirit! My son, strive for the finish line of holiness, the ribbon of gold, the crossing into Eternal Life for without effort you may fall and stumble, so maintain your speed, keep up the pace, don't look back, stay focused on the prize! Peter, My son, I love you, live in God's Will, love in God's Will, be united to the Trinity and you will cross the finish line into eternal bliss! Peace be with you."

"I love You, my King."

"...CARE NOT ABOUT YOURSELF SO I CAN CARE FOR YOU" April 7, 1994 AM 00:15

"My son, love says it all. It is the main topic and heading in the story of Creation. Love is the reason for creatures, love is the reason for the creation of the Earth and all its life. My son, energize your life for love of Me, do what is necessary and pleasing to others by your aid and caring in all their concerns. Offer a gentle word, a kind gesture. My Children have all been wounded, their lives hurt by mistrust. So, My son, love others, care not about yourself so I can care for you. Put all your attention into serving others by realizing that to love and serve others is to be Me, to imitate Me for that was the life I led. Peace be with you, My son, rest now in My Arms. "

"...LIVE IN AND DO MY WILL MOMENT BY MOMENT..." April 7, 1994 AM 10:15

"My son, blessed are those who live in and do My Will moment by moment for to live in this world is to be caught in the trap of confusion, of distractions, of wanderings, of anxiety. Only by living in the present moment will you be free from worries, troubles, cares, for all of these concerns are due to the creatures thinking about what may or could happen at some point in the future and God the Father controls the future. He wills and directs men's lives. His Plan is comprehensive, it is detailed, it is complex and to live in His Will is to know that the future is being taken care of fully and totally for the rest of your existence here on Earth and in the hereafter. My son, to live moment by moment is a school in trust, a school in abandonment, a school in confidence in the providence of God the Father, a school of dependence on My Love, a school in dying to your own desire to control and direct your own life by using your own will. So, My son, to live this way, only thinking about the present circumstances, the present situation, the present task at hand is very important in the development of your life in accordance with the Will of God which is your purpose, this school of being one with His Will. So, My son, have faith in your Dad, have faith in His Care, have faith in His Omnipotence, for He truly controls all things and He and I are One and We love you without measure and are making sure that every detail of your home and vocational life is turning out for your best interest so stop treading water, don't swim upstream, let My Hands support you and relax, live in peace, live in harmony, live as the rock on the ocean shore. Let it storm, let the waves crash on you but remain calm and serene and unmovable by living one minute to the next knowing that God loves you and He is in *control and making sure you are not being hurt or will not be hurt by creatures, the world or the devil unless it is for your growth in holiness in which case you will in the end be drawn closer to the Trinity and be the recipient of greater graces and additional insight and teaching of the Father's Will for your life. So now return to the world but only be concerned about the task at hand and do your best and I will take care of the rest. I love you, Peter, to the end of the Universe. I leave you in My Peace, in My Love and in My Heart."*

"I love You, my Lord, thank you."

"You are welcome, keep your head up and your hands folded and pray for souls."

"...SATAN IS ANGRY AND WANTS TO UPSET YOUR LIFE..." April 8, 1994 AM 06:45

"My son, take care to be at peace, to love sincerely, to dwell in My Heart, for Satan is angry and wants to upset your life, so stay close to Me and your Mother and We will guide and direct you each minute, each hour. I love you Peter, carry on with your activities, We go together."

"I love You, my Lord and trust in Your Love."

"...LOVE IS THE KINGDOM OF GOD" April 8, 1994 PM 00:00 (noon)

"My son, happy are those who love with joy, with peace, with humility, for theirs is the Kingdom of God! Happy are those who serve others, who help others, who give of themselves without expecting repayment, for theirs is the Kingdom of God! Happy are those who deny themselves, who sacrifice, who fast, who pray for their brother's and sister's salvation, for theirs is the Kingdom of God! Happy are those who care for the sick, care for the poor, care for the homeless, for theirs is the Kingdom of God! Happy are those who strive to be united to the Trinity with their whole heart, their whole mind, their whole soul, for theirs is the Kingdom of God! Happy are those who begin the day, begin the week, begin the

month with the goal to be in the Kingdom of God by being united to My Love, My Peace, My Joy in My Sacred Heart, for they will be kept there each day, each week, each month drowned in My Love, for I love them and Love is the Kingdom of God! Back now to your mission of love. I love you, My son."

"I love You, my King of My Heart."

"...THE FULFILLMENT OF MY PRAYER, THE PRAYER OF THE SON, THE 'OUR FATHER'" April 8, 1994 PM 11:00

"My son, blessed are those who live in and do My Will, for God the Father, God the Son and God the Holy Spirit are enraptured with joy, for the Divine Plan is fulfilled. In the beginning and after mankind fell, God the Father was sad, was discouraged with the human will of the creature, for He desired a human will that would die to itself and be born again with the Divine Will of the Father, a Will so perfect as to create a perfect image of Him within the creature. The Father desires a transformation of all human wills into the Divine Will. He desires a surrender of all human wills into the Father's Hands. My son, now is the time, now is the period that the Divine Will will reign in all creatures. It is the fulfillment of My Prayer, the Prayer of the Son, the 'Our Father'. So, My son, these are exciting times to live in and all are called but few are chosen. You have grown, My son, with the trials and tribulations of this life as have the others and in God's perfect Providence you have now a desire and appreciation of living in and doing God's Will. So unlike the first creatures, My Family will not have to choose, they will cling to the Divine Will, for after having seen what the result is of the human will dominating the Earth, they will only desire the Divine Will, for history has shown over and over again that men's affairs run by the human will result in chaos, confusion, disorder, greed, lust for power and control and all that blossoms out of the human will which is also influenced by the evil one. So, My son, rejoice to be

living in God's Holy Will, His Plan, His Design for Creation and be content in the thought that soon God the Father will fulfill the prayer of the Son and deliver the Earth's inhabitants from evil and then will come the new Era where all live in and do the Father's Will. Peter, have only these thoughts of the future, for as you know, this world is just about done and soon it will be so turned upside down that unless you hold onto the knowledge of God's Holy Plan for His Family you will be greatly troubled. So remain at peace, trust totally in the providence of God, surrender and abandon yourself without reserve, live moment by moment and be united to My Sacred Heart and to the Immaculate Heart of your Mother knowing that all is occurring for the total renewal of the Earth and to provide a new place, a new paradise where My Brothers and Sisters can live and raise families and worship the Trinity as God the Father desires and as such it will be done - FIAT. I love you Peter, we go together in peace, in love, in joy, in union with God's Holy Will."

"Thank You, my King."

"You're welcome, My Love for you does not end."

"I love You, Jesus."

"...I WANT TO TALK MORE ABOUT MY LOVE FOR YOU" April 9, 1994 PM 10:15

"My dear son, today is a day of remembrance, a day of rejoicing, a day to mark in the log of your life, for today occurred a happening that will change the hearts of many souls. It is the day that you began the way to publish and distribute the words I have given you. My son, Peter, as your brother said today, with this gift also comes the responsibility of acting and doing the Father's Will in regards to this gift and His Will is My Will and His Design for these messages is great, for they contain a great measure of instructions and directives in being a Soldier of Love, in being an Apostle of Love, in being a Son or Daughter of My Divine Will. They are words of hope for My Children, words of consolation for My

Children, words that will bring direction and purpose to their lives here on Earth and if followed will bring great glory for them in Heaven. My son, you were chosen for this mission in accordance with the direction of the Trinity, with the Fiat of the Father, Son and Holy Spirit. We have placed this mission in your care for its duration. My son, you are fortunate indeed to have been chosen and We intend to see it to completion. We will be with you always. We will aid you. We will direct you. Have no confidence in yourself, trust only in us for all your decisions, all your support, all your strength and persistence to follow through. My son, all things are possible with God and We are with you. My son, you will receive the gifts you require for this mission. You will be guided to persons that will join with you and assist you in every way, including financially. So have no concern, no anxiety, no fear, be a nothing, be abandoned, be surrendered. Turn it all over to Us and it will happen, all for the glory of God. Peter, desire only to live the way We have been teaching you, especially live moment to moment enveloped in Our Love, Our Peace, Our Joy. Now I want to talk more about My Love for you. Peter, you are a Son of My Divine Will. You have chosen this and made your consecration by and with your free will. This brings God the Father, God the Son and God the Holy Spirit and Mary your Mother exuberant joy. Thank you! We love you, We bless you, We embrace you in Our Arms. My son, you have made the consecration to Our Hearts, to the Holy Spirit. These too are very pleasing to Us. Thank you! We love you. My son, you are striving to live as we are asking, to learn and live in the Divine Will. Thank you! We love you, My son. When I say We love you, it represents a Love that is indescribable, a Love that is limitless, a Love that is beyond measure, a Love that is truly inconceivable in your limited mind. My son, if you could begin to comprehend this Love We have for you, you would never lose your peace, never lose your serenity, never not trust Us, for this Love is so great and God is so Great and controls all, that you should be totally content every minute of your life that everything that is happening to you is the perfect and best that could happen. So, My son, be a perfect Son of My Divine Will, be totally nothing, live in full union with the Trinity in one accord and as time passes, you will grow up, up, up to reach the height of sanctity, for We will raise you according to your desires and intention to live in and do the Will of God. Peter, fear not anything living or in the spirit world, fear not for your life or needs of this world, remain in total trust and knowledge that living in God's Will is total security and peace in all facets of your Earthly existence. My son, all We ask is love each moment of your life. We only want love, the love that resides in your heart, so be content, live simply, live a life of total commitment to love in all its forms and you will be blessed with Our Graces and Gifts. We will make you a lighthouse on the rocky shoreline of the ocean, We will use you personally and the words We have given you to bring souls home safely to the harbor even in the midst of the terrible storm. So reflect Our Light always with great brightness and you will be a beacon of hope, a light in the darkness, a way to the harbor of love and peace. Rest now, My son, in My Arms and let My Love be your future. I love you Peter."

"I love You, my Lord and my God."

"...THIS IS THE DAY OF MERCY..." April 10, 1994 AM 11:00

"My son, this is the day of mercy, the day to become aware of My Great Mercy, of My Great Capacity to forgive the sins of mankind, a day to be in prayer for mercy to triumph in the hearts of mankind. My son, all of mankind needs My Mercy. The world is sick with hate, with selfishness, with sin of every type and to every degree. The evil one has gone wild in his pursuit to rebel against God. Mankind has opened the window of their hearts and wills to his slavery and he has invaded them and is striving to destroy all of creation. My Mercy is the only answer. My Love is greater than his evil

and Love shall conquer for the evil one's plans shall be foiled and the Mercy of My Divine Heart will rescue the remnant and many others from his, the devil's, clutches. Mercy is love, is caring, is forgiveness and the Divine Mercy Devotion is for these times. So practice your faith, pray the chaplet and follow the devotional teachings. I bless you, My son, and I will be with you today. This day, so active, you will be placed with many families at the pine wood derby, so live My Teachings, be transparent, be nothing, love with the Love of God, the perfect Love of God. Wear My Smile, help anyway you can, listen to the hurting mothers, the hurting fathers, get on your knees with the children and console the losers and share in the joy of the winners. Be a bright light of love even on this sunny day. My son, family life is the hub, the center of the wheel of God's Plan, God's Design for mankind. It is where love is taught and practiced. It is the foundation of the lives of My Children so shine, My son, explode, My son, with the power of My Divine Love. Go now, prepare, be on your best behavior, no thoughts of self, only of others. I love you, My son, We go together in love, in peace, in joy."

"I love You, my Lord, thank you."

"You're welcome, let us go now."

"I NEED YOUR PRAYERS AND ALL OF MY CHILDREN'S" April 10, 1994 PM 11:20

"My child, this is your Mother, I love you, Jesus is My Lord and Savior, He is my all! My child, please pray for souls, pray with all your heart, all your strength. Peter, the evil one is running out of time and he is working overtime. He is dragging souls, thousands and thousands, to Hell each day, because not enough prayers are being said. My child, pray the Rosary, pray the Chaplet of Mercy, pray the unceasing 'Act of Love', offer up your day, all your work, all your activities. I need your prayers and all of my children's. My child, the Trinity is pleased with the actions you are taking to get these words out. They will aid many and will cause many prayers to be said so don't slow down, make it a priority. I am covering your flanks. Keep zeroed in, it is very important. My child, I am your Mother, come to me with your problems and cares and I will direct you as you discussed with N. the other day. I will always be there like your Earthly Mother was and my Heart is the Heart of a Perfect Mother created by God and given to you as a gift by Jesus on the cross. So fly to me and I will wipe your tears, I will console, I will understand, I will pray for you to the Father. Peter, as Jesus revealed to you today through N., you are an Apostle of these Last Days and I will guide you and encourage you in your mission as I did the first Apostles and members of my Son's Body. I am asking that God the Holy Spirit pour out upon you more gifts and I desire only that you be satisfied completely and totally with God's Will. Peter, the day is done and you must rest to be ready for tomorrow's mission so fall asleep in my arms. I am going to protect you as a bear protects her baby cubs."

"I love you, my Mother, my dear Mother."

"...LIVE AND PRACTICE THE DIVINE WILL TEACHINGS..." April 11, 1994 AM 6:15

"My son, blessed are those who live and practice the Divine Will Teachings, for they shall receive grace from Heaven above, for their efforts go not unnoticed and their prayers are surely heard. The Father listens with great joy and gives His Fiat for their growth in the learning and experiencing the Wisdom of His Knowledge, the Wisdom of His Kingdom, the Wisdom of the Creator, for the Divine Will Teachings are new and uplifting, are fresh and full of the Divine Wisdom and Knowledge and all those who study and grasp this new way please the Trinity greatly. My son, pray also to be full of God's Holy Spirit, to be a child of the Trinity, a child that lives in the Kingdom, a child of great understanding of the Father's Will, for blessed is His Will, it is Wisdom, it is Love and all that are His Divine Will Children are united into the Family of God, are united into the Kingdom *of His Love, are united with the Fiat of the Father, Son, and Holy Spirit and the Fiat of the Blessed Virgin. My son, be filled with My Holy Spirit, be filled with the graces and gifts from Him, that you may be a light in the darkness, a beacon of hope, a channel of God's gifts to His lost Children, to His troubled Children, to His own Children, for He loves His Children and wants all His Children to come home, come home to His Land of Love, His Land of Peace, His Land of Joy, His Land where the Trinity can completely transform their lives into images of Themselves, for God the Father desires a unity of spirit, of mind, of will in all His Creation and His Will will be done - FIAT. Peter, strive for holiness, strive for oneness, strive for unity, strive for complete conformity with the Divine Will. Live as We have been teaching, practice and be transformed into a child of the Divine Will. My Blessing is upon you, My Spirit is upon you, My Will is in you. Now begin the day with new vigor, new strength, new purpose to be one with the Trinity. I love you, My son, to the depth of the ocean."*

"I love You, my Lord and my God."

"...TO LIVE IN AND TO DO HIS WILL ARE DIFFERENT..." April 11, 1994 PM 02:30

"My dear son, this is your Mother. I would like to speak to you today about doing the Father's Will. Peter, as you know, to live in His Will is the best of the best. Well, to live in and to do His Will are different in that you know what to do at each moment by living in His Will, so to do His Will is actions and activities but to live in His Will is a state of being, an attitude, a frame of mind. Life in His Will is maintaining His Peace, His Serenity. It is not being troubled, not being upset about the past or future or having or not having or pleasing or not pleasing creatures. It is living moment by moment in a state of loving the Trinity, in a state of total dependence, total abandonment, total surrender and total confidence in your Father's Will. My child, if you are

living in His Will then you will be inspired to do His Will, for His Will is doing the right, the just, the best thing in every circumstance, in every situation that you are placed in with your brothers and sisters. It is living the truths and directives of the Gospel and the true church. It is imitating Christ my Son to the full and complete extent. My dear child, to add to this is to be consecrated to the Divine Will which means you have no will of your own, you only do God's Holy Will. To live in God's Holy Will with God's Holy Will as your own will is to be united to the Creator, it is to be one with His Directives, it is to fit perfectly into His Divine Plan for the salvation of mankind and to begin to live a life as will be lived in the new Era and as is lived in Heaven. Only God's Will exists, only His Directives are followed, only His Plan is implemented. My dear child, how fortunate you are to have this teaching. In addition to having God's Will, you also have consecrated yourself to my Heart, to my Son's Heart and to the Holy Spirit. This means that you have joined your heart to Our Hearts and your spirit to God's Spirit. Your drop has become part of the ocean of the love contained in Our Hearts and the ocean of virtues contained in Our Hearts. Your spirit has become united to the Spirit of God. So, my dear child, you have the Will of the Father, the Spirit of God, the Heart of God and the Heart of Mary, your Mother. These are all helping you to do God's Will. The only hindrance is the world, the flesh and the devil, so you must stay committed, you must not slacken, you must press on and implement Our Teachings to you, Our Directives to you and with the Grace of God you will become a Son of the Divine Will, tall, strong and robust, full of holy zeal, full of the love of God and Neighbor, full of all virtues and the Holy Will of God will reign and you will reflect the Light of Christ and the Peace of the Holy Spirit and you will blossom with love for your brothers and sisters. So, my dear child, have no will of your own, let God's Will reign, have no heart, let my Son's and my Heart reign, have no spirit, let His Spirit possess you fully and totally and do the perfect, just and right Will of God every second, every minute of each day. Return now to your activities in the world but stay focused on your mission of love. I love you, my dear Son of the Father's Will. "

"I love you, my dear, loving Mother, my Mommy. Thank you for your teaching, please pray that I may make them a part of my life and being. "

"I Will, my little one, I will, go now and do your work. "

"...THE DIVINE WILL WILL BE ESTABLISHED ON EARTH AS IT IS IN HEAVEN... " April 11, 1994 PM 11:40

"My dear child, this is your Mother. Jesus is My Lord and Savior, my All. Thank you, my child, for desiring to get these words out, thank you for the joy of your heart, thank you for the love you showed to others. My dear Son of the Divine Will, be enveloped in the Love of God from the instant you wake up to the moment you fall asleep. Be a torch of love in a hate-filled world, a selfish world, a confused world. It will all change soon! It will be a terrible storm but through it all will remain my children of my Heart for I will protect and lead them to the meeting with my Son. He will come and reign as King and I will reign as Queen and the world will be renewed, the Divine Will will be established on Earth as it is in Heaven, for the Lord God has proclaimed it and it will be done. My dear child, the Fiat of the Father is in agreement with the decree of the Father, Son and Holy Spirit, for God's Will is one and the same for Father, Son and Holy Spirit. My dear child, God's Holy Will will be done and the Father is running this schedule and the schedule is indicating that time is very short before this world will go through the Great Trials and when they begin, all will be in turmoil, all will be affected by God's Holy Wrath. He is sweeping out His House to clean it so He can remake it and have a place that His children can grow strong in the Faith and live in His Will. It will be as He Wills and His Will is final. My child, strive with all your

32

might and be dedicated to learning about and living in the Divine Will for it is the future and it will make the trial period a period of joy because you will know what is next, the total rebirth of mankind - God's Creation, living as He Designed in a new World, fresh and clean in both the physical and spiritual, for Satan will be chained and the Earth will be renewed. So, my son, live in joyful expectation and know that all that is occurring is in God's Hands and He loves us to no end. I love you, my little Child in the Divine Will!"

"I love you Mom, thank you."

"You're welcome."

"...THE GARDEN OF THE DIVINE WILL..." April 12, 1994 AM 10:15

"My dear child, please take my hand as I walk in the Garden of the Will of God. It is a Divine Garden. It is a Garden where great souls are raised. It is a Garden where peace is the rule, love is the rule. It is a Garden where seeds are planted in the soil of the hearts of men and women and great flowers sprout forth with many blossoms and each blossom is a virtue and each branch is a direct route to the heart where love flows and keeps the flower full of color, full of life, full of freshness. It is a Garden where the hearts are united with roots to the living water, the source of life and nourishment, the Will of God. For all stems from God's Fiat and all are full of God's Love that live in the Garden of the Will of God. Oh what beautiful walks I can now take in this Garden where all my souls are growing and the heavenly aroma is magnificent from all the flowers. The love comes and forms a mist of aroma that can melt a heart of stone into a heart of fine soil that can be placed in the Garden of His Will and in this Garden there are no weeds, no thieves stealing the flowers for this Garden is a Garden in the new Era, a Garden where no reprobates are allowed. No evil devils are allowed to enter, only the heavenly Angelic workers. They nurture and plow around the roots, they hold up and tie the branches for it

is the Father's Garden now in its entirety and we all want to do His Will and live in His Divine Garden. Oh what a place, oh what a paradise! Oh what a dream come true, the Garden of the Divine Will, the place where all my children, my sons and daughters of My Heart, of the Father's Will, will live after the storm, after the trial. I love you, my special child of the Father's Will, continue on your mission of love. "

"I love you, my mom, thank you for that walk in the garden!"

"You are welcome. Go now and do your work for souls. "

"...LIVING IN GOD'S WILL IN THE NEW ERA WILL BE THE REIGN OF LOVE OF ALL HEARTS" April 12, 1994 PM 11:15

"Blessed are those who seek to dwell in the bosom of the Father's Embrace, in His Arms, close to His Heart. They seek the Love of the Father, the Love of God, the Love of the Most High. It is their only desire, their only objective in life, their only happiness, for they will have their fill, for God's Love will surround them as the air they breathe and it will consume them in flames of radiant heat, the heat of the love of the Creator. For all God desires from His Creatures is their love. It is the reason they were created, the reason they exist. Oh what a desire the Father has for our love, not for a selfish love, not for an insincere love, but for a love that is pure, that is from the heart. God the Father is a God of Love, not hate. God the Father is a God of Peace, not war. God the Father is a God of Truth, not deception. My dear child, the Father's Will is divine, it is endless, it has no capacity to be overruled by the creature, for it is omnipotent and His Will is to love the creature with all His Love, sparing none. For the Father is the Creator of Love itself, it is where love was conceived, where love had its beginning, where love had its source, for if the creature will open up his heart to invite the Love of God in then God the Father will make of it another spring of His Love, *a new source that can in return love the Father and love his neighbor and love will flow between creatures, between hearts and where there is love there is God and where there is God resides His Will, for God wills the creature to love Him and all those the creature comes in contact with, with His Love, the Love from His Heart, the Love of His Own, the Divine Love of God the Father, God the Son and God the Holy Spirit. If the creature can not hinder the love from flowing, not hinder the unity of love between creatures, then God's Love can reign in the hearts of all men and will flow between all men and all will be enraptured with the love of God and the love of neighbor. This is God's Will and to live in God's Will is to be transparent by being a nothing, having no desires, living for each moment, pleasing not creatures, being at peace. And living in God's Will in the new Era will be the reign of love of all hearts. It will be a plague of love. All will catch it and it will consume all and there will be union of all hearts in the bond of love as all will live in the Will of the Father. So, My Son of My Father's Will, of My Will, begin today to let love flow in greater proportions by living the teaching and you will begin living the life of the new Era, the life where love will flow from all hearts. I love you, My son, with the love of the brightness of the Sun."*

"I love You, my Lord of Love, please bless me with the grace to be a nothing and live in Your Will."

"I will, My son, live your heart's intentions."

"...MY WILL IS THAT HE STOP DRINKING COMPLETELY" April 13, 1994 AM 05:50

"My son, tell N. he must go to confession, that he does overdrink and needs the strength, the grace from My Sacrament to overcome this weakness. Tell him to place this sin at My Feet and not to depend on his strength to overcome it, for it is much indwelt in his being and only by depending on My Strength will he overcome it. Tell him to fast and pray and offer up the denial of his drinking to save souls and it will save

many. *It will be a great glory to God, it will be a great defeat to the evil one who laughs and enjoys each time he brings drinks to his lips. Tell him he must end this drinking for it is hurting his growth in holiness and the love in his family. My son, I love N. as I love you and want this slavery to end. Thank him for Me for his work and his desire to please Me. Tell him that My Will is that he stop drinking completely.*"

"...ALWAYS STAY ABANDONED IN THE WILL OF THE FATHER" April 14, 1994 AM 01:00

"My dear son, living in the Will of the Father is peace, is joy, is living in the state of abandonment to God's Providence, for to live in His Will is to know that all is being taken care of and nothing has been left to chance. His Will controls the material, it controls the physical, it controls the spiritual and to live in His Will is harmony with all three. It is to be as a buoy on the ocean channel that drifts with the tide, floating and bobbing yet anchored to the ocean floor. The buoy is affected by the ocean current only to the extent of the tidal changes for it does not float away with the current changes, only rests secure, being a marker for the ships traveling the ocean, guiding and directing them in their journey to the harbor of calm waters, the harbor of peace, where rest and recovery can take place and rebuilding can be done in the calm, still waters. My son, to live in My Will is to be a ship in this harbor of peace tied to the dock, secure from all storms. Living in His Will is peace, for God the Father is controlling the schedule of life's activities. He sets the time for work, for play. He manages the activities so that time may be saved yet all accomplished, for God the Father controls all, manages all, directs all and assures all that live in His Will that all is peace and joy. For being abandoned to God's Will is to be controlled by the One who knows all, sees all and directs all. My son, it is easy to be at peace in any of life's circumstances when you know everything is being taken care of and so it is with God's Will. He is taking care of all of the occurrences on

a micro scale and a macro scale for each life on this Earth. He is taking care of all the occurrences of weather and all other physical changes that take place in our lives. He is in control of all the spiritual activities that are occurring so to live in God's Will is to be in harmony with all and to know that you are just here to live in and do God's Will and as such peace can reign and joy can reign in our lives for we are anchored in the stable and immovable ocean floor, we are tied to the secure docks, protected in the safe harbor. We are not concerned about time for there is time for all important activities to occur and we know that being guided by the director of all that all will be accomplished in peace and joy, completely and totally in harmony with everything, if we don't block it with our will but always stay abandoned in the Will of the Father. Rest now, My son, and fall back in the Arms that support you, direct you and care for you each second of every day now and for all eternity. I love you, My son, peace and joy be yours."

"I love You, my King, my Lord, my God."

"...MY WILL IS HAVING ALL OF THESE TRAITS..."
April 14, 1994 AM 06:00

"My son, to live in My Will is to fill your heart with goodness, justice, equality and all that begets love, for My Will is all these and infinitely more and to live in My Will is to be united to these and other qualities of the Creator, for to live in My Will is to fill your heart with a storehouse of character and virtuous attributes. My son, living in My Will is having all of these traits, all of these gifts infused into your heart by proxy, for God the Father desires a heart that is made in His Image in all creatures and His Will be done - FIAT - for the new Era will be an Era of order, of harmony, an Era of error free living, an Era where all goodness flows from all hearts and is nurtured and strengthened in the school of life to love God the Father, Son and Holy Spirit and love your neighbor with the Heart of your God. Another day begins now, live moment by

37

moment, just put one step in front of another and love, love, love. I love you, My son."

"I love You, my Lord and God."

"...A SON OR DAUGHTER LIVING IN THE DIVINE WILL MUST KNOW THAT TO FULFILL THEIR DAILY DUTIES IS GOD'S WILL FOR THEIR LIFE..." *April 14, 1994 AM 12:00*

"My dear son, happy are those who fulfill their obligations in this life, for they will be glorified in the next. The obligations of this life are many but one must always be focused on only those that are a part of the Father's Plan, the Father's Will for their state or vocation that has been assigned them. My son, a son or daughter living in the Divine Will must know that to fulfill their daily duties is God's Will for their life, for work is a blessing and if done with joy and peace can glorify the Father in many ways. For the Father of a family as you are, it is a work for love, it is to provide shelter and to meet the needs of your wife and those precious children that have been placed in your care. Work is a prayer, it is a sacrifice and can be offered up to save souls. Work is a ministry, for with your work, My son, Jesus can use all your faculties to plant seeds and love souls, those souls that are placed in your path by the providence of the Father. So, my son, love your work, be thankful for your work, for it is a gift from the Father. My dear son, you must work hard and you must do your work well, however, you must keep it separate from your family and spiritual life. You must be able to live moment by moment and thereby not mix them or overlap them, for if you do, you will do poorly in all and have much unrest and be full of anxiety. My dear child, you must control your expenditures and live very simply for God will not provide for your needs if they are not necessary or not needed for your existence here on Earth. My dear child, your vocation has been chosen for you in order that you can be a Soldier of Love, an Apostle of Love, for so many souls are headed for the abyss

and those you work with or will work with are in need of your prayers and sacrifices and example. So always be sure to trust completely in Us for all your needs and be not troubled about anything that occurs in your work life for We are using your work life to raise you up in the Divine Will, raise you up in a school of trust, in a school of abandonment, in a school of total dependence on Our Love for you. So always stay at peace and use every opportunity to love and live united to the Divine Will in all your activities and We will be with you in all that you do and all that you are with as you pass your time here in the world living abandoned to the Father's Will. I love you, My dear Son of My Father's Will."

"I love you, my Queen and Mother, my Mom."

"...WITH THE CONSECRATION TO THE DIVINE WILL YOU ARE UNITED TO THE TRINITY..." April 14, 1994 PM 10:00

"My dear child, blessed are those who strive to be united with the Trinity in all they say and do, for love resides there, love has its throne there, love is encapsulated there in the Heart of God. My dear child, to be united to the Trinity means you are one with the Father, Son, Holy Spirit in all ways. You have the Heart of God, the Wisdom of the Father and the Graces of the Spirit. To be united to the Trinity you have God's Holy Will and you live at all times doing His Holy Will, for He is running the command post of your being, He is running the source of your strength, the heart of your soul, the life of your body. He controls all and is tuned with the happenings and details of your daily life. My dear child, union with the Trinity is the greatest gift, for it is being united to pure love, united to pure wisdom, to the Will of God, and as such you can then love with the Love of God, be wise with the Wisdom of the Father and always live in and do the Will of God, all for the glory of the Trinity. My dear child, living in the Divine Will is so important, for to live in His Will, consecrated to His Will, you are united to the Trinity and to

live in His Will you must follow His Teachings and mine, that of being a nothing, no attachments to creatures or material things, living abandoned, surrendered and dependent, with full trust in your Lord and not even the thought of sin. So, my child, with the consecration to the Divine Will you are united to the Trinity, so strive to live in God's Will and all of the Trinity's Qualities will expound[1] from your being. My dear child, I will be helping you to live in the Divine Will. I will raise you up to higher heights, for I am your Mother and it brings me great joy to teach and build my child in the ways of the Father, Son and Holy Spirit. This is my duty, this is my way of pleasing the Trinity, so please try with all of your heart to live the teachings and depend on me to raise you up and teach you the ways of our God. I love you Peter, abandon yourself to my motherly care."

"I love you, my Mother, my Sweet Mom."

"BE A MEEK AND HUMBLE LAMB TO ALL, NEVER GET ANGRY..." April 15, 1994 PM 01:20

"My son, happy are those who love without measure, for theirs is the Kingdom of God. A meek heart is special in God the Father's Eyes, for love has its root in meekness and God desires all His Sons and Daughters to share in the Meekness of the Savior, for He did not complain, He did not become bitter, He did not become upset in any way with the Passion of His Death on the cross. Be a meek and humble lamb to all, never get angry, always know that the providence of God is placing you in circumstances and situations to use you and set examples to others of how to be a Christ in the world. Know that all things work out for your good and God's Will must be the only desire you have, to fulfill It, to live in It, to do It with love, peace and joy for the Glory of the Trinity.

---

[1] This seems to say that Peter's being will somehow explain, interpret, or unfold the Trinity's Qualities. The word 'expound' is defined as 'to explain, to interpret, to unfold'.

Back to your mission of love, My son, I love you and embrace you and go with you, let us go."

"I love You, my King."

"...YOU WILL BE TAKEN CARE OF" April 15, 1994 PM 11:00

"My son, another day has passed, another day closer to the new Era. Continue to prepare by living and practicing My and My Mother's Teaching to you. My son, how can you be sure that you are doing your best? Well, My son, always stay united to the Heart of your Mother for she is the special instrument of these last days that will conquer evil and deliver the children of the Father's Will through the storm to the new Era. My son, be content in the fact that you and your family are living to please Me the best you can and therefore you will be taken care of. Many changes will occur. There will be much hardship but you are on the winning team and will be guided and protected for I love you My son who is striving to love Me and do My Will and therefore you need not concern yourself but live each day, each moment abandoned to My Will, loving, praying and striving to please the Father. I love you, My child."

"I love You, my Jesus."

"...LIVING IN HIS WILL IS THE BEST OF THE BEST..."
April 16, 1994 AM 05:35

"My dear child, to live in the Will of the Father is joy without end, for all is accomplished through His Will, with His Will, in His Will and His Will is order, harmony and peace, My dear child, for living in His Will is to be in a haven protected from all that could upset and harm and living in His Will is living in union with all of creation, for all of creation is already living in His Will. My dear child, being a Son or Daughter of the Father's Will means you are ready to follow the Lord wherever it is His Pleasure to go and living in His Will is the best of the best for to be united to the Mind of the

Creator is to be in union with the Supreme Commander of all things living and not living. His Will is goodness itself and living in His Will is where all decisions are made for all that happens now and in the future, for the Fiat of the Father is final and not being united to the Creator, creatures are at odds with all of creation. So, My dear child, being a Child of God, the Father's Will is the ultimate goal for all creatures. The creature must surrender his will without reserve, he must die to his will, he must have no will of his own and he must invite God's Holy Will to fill the void and replace his own. This is a process of death and at the same time new life, to kill your human will is to always do God's Holy Will. It is to be far from and completely separate from sin, it is to be grounded in love of God and neighbor and follow and imitate the life of My Lord and Savior Jesus Christ, Son of God. My dear child, to live each moment is to deny your will for your will wants to be in control of your future and not to trust in God the Father's providence. To be obedient to other's commands is to deny your will, for your will wants to make all the decisions, to run and rule in your own life and in others. Now without your own will, you will be living in the Divine Will, for God the Father's Will will be calling all the shots and God's Will will always make all the right decisions and His Will is ruling in you now because you have made your consecration to His Will. So you must always be sure that His Will is leading you in this way, in all your acts and activities of this life. You must constantly place in your mind the commitment and desire to let His Will reign by asking that His Will reign in you and ask to be inspired by His Holy Will and God the Father will hear your prayer and will reign and you will as time passes spend life here on Earth living in and doing God's Will each instant, your ultimate goal. You must go now and prepare to receive. My son, I love you. My dear child, continue on your mission of love."

"I love you, my Mom, my Mommy."

"My son, how happy I was today with My Family, striving to learn and understand the Divine Will Teachings. So was Luisa, for her effort was to bring the teachings to the family members in these last days especially. There is a lot to learn, so press on My son. I would like to talk to you about My Will tonight. My Will is God the Father's Plan for His Family (At this time, I fell asleep in my chair. When I awoke, my arm was limp)."

"My dear son, I love you. I am in control of everything. Please don't be concerned about your arm, I am in control. Let us continue to talk about My Will. My Will is the Father's Will. It is Perfect. It is without flaw. It controls everything. It is My Most Precious Gift for My children. It is what I saved to this point of time to give to My children, for I love My children. My Will is grace. With the creature's consent, it replaces his or her own will, and if nurtured, and if the creature continues to hinder his or her own will from ruling, then My Will will rule in the creature, then My Will will be done in that creature's life. For My Will is power, for with My Fiat anything is accomplished, for I am God. To live in accordance with My Will is to please Me greatly, it is to please Me to the ultimate extent the creature can please Me, for I desire all of My Creatures to have My Holy Will in them, in place of their own human will. And if the creature will accept My Will, and consecrate themselves to My Divine Will, I will truly reign in that creature with My Will and all its attributes. It will live in My Will. It will have peace. It will be serene. It will live a carefree life, yet a productive life in this world and in saving souls, for it will not waste any of its time, for living in My Will and doing My Will is living your life to the greatest degree possible in the most efficient manner here on this Earth. It is not to waste any time. It is always to be using your time wisely, perfectly, and in accordance with

My Father's Plan. It is to always have peace, it is to always have joy of heart. It is to be always glorifying the Father, the Son, the Holy Spirit. It is to live according to My Fiat. Once the consecration has been made, it is so important to continue, to repeat the ejaculation of My Will reigning in your life ('Divine Will, come and reign in me!'). It is so important to keep this in front of you as your main purpose, as your main directive in your life. For creatures are weak, creatures are in the flesh. Creatures have not the mind of God. So they have to continue to discipline themselves in thoughts and words as well as actions. But with My Will, My Divine Will infused and replacing the creature's will in the creature, the creature can reach a more perfected state, if the creature strives with his heart or her heart to reach this state. He or she will grow as time passes, grow to live in and do the Will of the Father, and this will please the Father, this will please the Son, this will please the Holy Spirit, this will please the Blessed Virgin Mary. For this is the new plan for the new Era. This is God's Will for mankind. This has always been God's Will for mankind and now God's Will will be fully implemented - FIAT. My son, I love you, I am in control of everything, please carry your cross, this inconvenience with your arm. Carry it well, carry it with joy. It is your cross, it is designed for you, and all things work out for the good of those that love Me. Abandon yourself, surrender yourself to My Divine Providence. I love you very much, My son. Now begin to prepare for Mass, for I am waiting. "

"I love You, my Jesus."

"...LIVE IN THE PRESENT MOMENT" April 17, 1994 PM 12:30

"My dear son, don't think about the past, don't think about the future, live in the present moment. For in the present moment is My Peace. It resides there. In the present moment, you can become lost in My Love for you. You can offer up the unceasing 'Act of Love'. You can ask for God's

44

Will to reign in you. *You can be one with Me and one with the Divine Will. By doing My Will, by asking for My Will to reign in you, you can be full of love, My Love for you, My Love for others. You can live in the Immaculate Heart of Mary, a heart of purity. You can be protected by the Immaculate Heart, protected from the evil one, enclosed in her Heart. Oh My son, live the present moment! Venture not into the future, think not of the past. Live only for the moment! Be full of joy and peace and love and gentleness and kindness. Be lost in My Love. Oh My son, I love you and want you to be full of this Love! I want you to be full of hope, hope in the future! I want you to have no fear, for I have you in My Hands, I have your life in My Hands! I will care for all your needs, I will care for your well being! I will only let you be affected by crosses that will benefit you. All of the crosses that I give you benefit you. Nothing will happen to you that will hurt you. Please let these words sink deep into your heart so that you might live the moment and not be concerned of anything of the future, and not be concerned of anything creatures say or do that affects you. Do not be concerned of any material needs or wants. My son, please meditate on the depth of My Love for you, for it does not end. My Peace be with you, My son. Back now to your study, and My Spirit will inspire you and teach you in the ways of the Divine Will. I love you Peter."*

"I love You, my King."

"...BECOME FULL OF THE WISDOM OF THE DIVINE WILL..." April 17, 1994 PM 03:15

"My dear child, I love you, this is your Mother. Please grasp my teaching of the book that you are reading ('The Virgin Mary in the Kingdom of the Divine Will'). Please be open to my words. Please empty your mind of all of your thoughts and the distractions of the world. Please read the entire book, for I meant this book to be read by you and all of my children of my Heart. My dear son Peter, I love you and I want you to become full of the Wisdom of the Divine Will

teachings so that you may become a child of the Divine Will to the fullest sense. I love you Peter. Take my hand and we will sit in the garden and I will instruct you with the words of the book. I love you. Go now and study and let it sink to the depths of your being. Be a nothing, so that the Holy Spirit can fill you with the Wisdom and the Teachings of the Will of God."

"I love you, my Mother."

"HAVE THIS PEACE SO THAT YOU MIGHT LIVE IN MY WILL..." April 18, 1994 AM 08:00

"My dear son, live in My Peace today. Be full of My Joy, be My Special Child, My Messenger of My Peace, of My Calmness, of My Serenity. Have this peace so that you might live in My Will, so that you might be able to practice and implement My Teachings. My son, I love you very much and desire you to become a Son of My Will. Thank you for your effort! Repeat the unceasing act ('Jesus, Mary, I love You, save souls'). Repeat the desire to have God's Will reign ('Divine Will, come and reign in me'). Repeat the act of humility ('I am nothing, God is everything'). And live in peace, do your daily duties as they are required for your vocation but do them with peace, and be sure to spend the whole day in My Will fulfilling your mission of loving all those you come in contact with by letting Me shine through. I love you, My son, I am waiting for you at Mass."

"I love You, my Jesus, straight-a-way."

"I WANT A PERFECT RELATIONSHIP WITH YOU" April 18, 1994 AM 09:20

"My dear son, as I was telling you at communion, you are on a special mission. The words I have given you are important and they need to be distributed as soon as possible to the far reaches of the world. They are part of the bringing in of the Kingdom. My son, I am taking care of all your needs, everything. Do not doubt this. Go forward without

*wasting any time. I will assist you, I will give you the graces
necessary. My son, I also need you because I want you to love
Me. I have so few people, children, that love Me. I want a
perfect relationship with you. I want you to live in My Will
and be My son, and to have a special relationship with Me and
with My Father and with the Holy Spirit and with the Virgin
Mary, My Mother. There are so few in this world that are not
all wrapped up in something, the worldly activities or
themselves, or the future or the past, or their activities. They
are all wrapped up. So son, be special, be focused, be focused
on carrying out your mission and loving Us. Have not a care.
Please don't get wrapped up in your work or what people think
of you, or pleasing people, others, so that you can remain
close to Us. I love you My son. Go now and do your daily
duties with Me. I am with you in all that you do, I love you
Peter."*

"I love You, my King."

***"...TO LIVE IN THE FATHER'S WILL YOU MUST
ACCEPT MARY'S PLACE IN THE PLAN.."** April 18, 1994
PM 10:00*

*"My son, tonight I would like to tell you of the love I
have for all My Children who dwell in the Heart of My Mother
by being consecrated to her Immaculate Heart. My son, the
Children of My Mother's Heart are very special to Me. They
are like close family members to Me, for they accept My
Mother with love, with care for her feelings, the feelings of her
Heart. My Mother is the most special creature in My Eyes, my
Eyes of Love, for she raised Me, she cared for Me, she was a
Perfect Mother to Me. She was also the Perfect Creature who
always did the Will of the Father. My Mother is hurt by all the
rejection of her separated children. These children are ones
that have been deceived by the evil one, for how could anyone
reject a gift from Jesus if they claim to be followers of Mine
except they have been deceived by the evil one? Oh My son,
pray for all the separated brothers and sisters. You will*

witness their enlightenment soon. It will be great, for Scripture must be fulfilled. There will be one fold and one shepherd. My son, blessed are those who love My Mother, for all the love that is given to her by creatures she gives to Me for Mary My Mother is in Heaven and in Heaven all are living in God's Will and Mary is a perfect Christian and gives all Praise, Honor and Glory to God the Father, Son, and Holy Spirit. My dear son, to love My Mother is to love Me, for how can a perfect son not love a perfect mother and how can My Divine Will not grant Mary what she desires? Oh My son, do not hesitate to love My Mother. I have given her to you as a gift, a powerful gift. She can guard you and nourish you in the Teachings of My Will. She can protect you and guide you in the upcoming events. My son, she is the woman of Genesis. She will crush the head of Satan. This is her mission in accordance with the Divine Will. My son, happy are those who love Mary and strive to imitate her and let her Heart reign through their hearts. Again I say, love My Mother for you are My Brother and God the Father is your Father and the Holy Spirit is your Sanctifier. You are a member of My Family so let Mom teach you and raise you in the Divine Will and she will do it for it is God's Will - FIAT. Peter, let us take a hike in the Kingdom, a walk in the Meadow of God's Holy Paradise, for there in the Meadow we will find our Mother with all her children. She is teaching them the way to the Father's Heart, she is teaching them how to die to their will and sweep their house clean so God's Holy Will can reign in its place. My son, to live in the Father's Will you must accept Mary's place in the Plan of Salvation for mankind, for if God the Father wants something done, it will be done and if God the Father wills to use Mary then Mary will be used. I love you, My son, continue striving to live and do His Will, for it is the end of the rainbow and there We are waiting to give you Our blessing and encouragement to press on and be filled with the Will of the Father, the Life, the Light, the Love of your soul. Peace, My son, rest now and I will rest too in your heart."

"I love You, my King."

"Thank you, please kiss Mom for Me and give her a big hug."

"I will, my Brother, goodnight."

"...HAVE YOU BEGUN TO REALIZE WHAT IS IN STORE FOR YOU AND THE OTHERS IN THE NEW ERA?" *April 19, 1994 AM 06:00*

"My dear son, have you begun to realize what is in store for you and the others in the new Era? It is going to be a life without sin, without evil, without hate. My son, it will be a time of refreshing, a time of renewal, a time of rebirth. It is going to be a reign of love, a reign of peace, a reign of joy. All will be full of the Spirit of God and they will be living in and doing the Will of God at all times because all will have no will of their own but all will have God's Holy Will dwelling in them. It will be their life, it will be their anchor, it will be their prize possession. My son, do you know that all will change, the Earth will be renewed with new life and the surface of the Planet will be resplendent to reflect the joy of the Trinity with the Will finally being established in the creature. My son, this is your future, this is the future of all those who strive and persevere to do God's Will, to live in God's Will, to be a Child of God in all ways. Rejoice, My son, for what is in store for the future will be truly stupendous, truly unimaginable, truly representative of God's Love for His Creatures and the care He desires to provide for His Family! So, My son, begin to live in this new Paradise by living as We have been teaching and you will begin to enjoy the fruits of God's Love for you, a constant peace, joy and contentment in doing God's Holy Will. Be one with the Trinity each moment and lose your will, your desires, your wants, your cares, your life in the vast ocean of God's Love. Go now, begin your mission of love. I love you, My Son of My Will."

"I love You, my King, my Lord, my Savior."

"...STEP BACK FROM THE WORLD BY LIVING ONE MOMENT AT A TIME..." *April 19, 1994 PM 01:15*

"My son, yes, your mind is all wrapped up in the world, for you have not perfected living one moment at a time, so keep striving to. My son, life in My Will is the goal and you can reach it! Stay focused and I will help you Peter. I love you and want you to be in the Will, with the Will, doing the Will, being united to the Will and reflecting and meditating how awesome the Will is! So step back from the world by living one moment at a time, loving Me and living in My Will and you will grasp the goal to be reached. Now go do your duties, go do them with love and go to your meeting and remember it is not the job, the world's tasks that is important, it is the placement and detonation and explosion of the Divine Love that will occur if you go as My Soldier and not as yourself. I love you, My son, We go together, peace."

"I love You, my King."

"...SLEEP IS A GIFT OF LOVE FROM THE FATHER" *April 19, 1994 PM 10:20*

"Goodnight, My son, sleep tight, My son, in the arms of My Love, tight in the bond of My Mother's love for you. Sleep, My son, and We will rest also in your heart, for sleep is a gift of love from the Father. Let your last thoughts, your last words be ones of love for Us. I love you, My son."

"I love You, my King."

"...STRIVE TO LIVE MOMENT BY MOMENT..." *April 20, 1994 AM 05:30*

"My dear son, today will be special for you, for today you will receive a multitude of My Graces from Father, so rejoice and remember with gifts come responsibilities. Thank you, My son, for your efforts. I love you Peter. Continue to strive to live moment by moment without cares of the future or past. Live in My Love and love Me and love souls. All else

is passing, all else is temporary. I will care for all your needs. Just be patient and trust in this regard. My son, please love Me more by thinking about Me instead of your work life of the future. Do your daily duties and then forget them. Don't think about the work you have to do way out in the future. My son, if you could only live moment by moment you would experience such joy, peace and serenity so please try harder. Here is your Mother, Peter."

"I am with you also, I reside in your heart with your Lord and My Lord and Savior Jesus, the King, so please talk to me and love me more also! We want to use you more so you must develop a close relationship with us so you can be more effective in your missions of love and in your prayer life. I love you, my child, and need you to be a special instrument in the battle that is now well underway, so continue to strive to live as We have been teaching and especially live moment to moment. Peter, live in the plane above the world, live in Heaven yet still on Earth in Our Hearts, in God's Will, be possessed by the Holy Spirit. You must clear away yourself if you desire this so live without care of yourself, for we are taking care of everything, just love Us and love souls. This is all We ask Peter, you will have crosses but please understand, each one you receive is for your best interest so embrace them and this includes your financial problems, so don't worry, don't doubt but trust and hope, for you are not in control of anything but God is and He loves you and would not let a fly land on you if it would hurt you so lose yourself in Our Love for you and live the teachings and you will see great progress in your spiritual life and in your state of mind being one of peace, love and joy. We love you, my dear Child of the Father's Will, now begin the mission and keep in touch all day. We want a much closer relationship." "I love you Mom..Jesus"

"I love you Mom. I love You, Jesus."

"...BE ONE WITH MY SPIRIT FOR MY SPIRIT IS LOVE..." April 20, 1994 PM 07:40

"My son, today is a day to be united to My Heart, My Will, My Mother. It is a day like all days, for this is your vocation, this is your purpose, this is your life, your life of the spirit, for the Holy Spirit is your best friend, your guide, your comforter. My son, to be united to My Heart, My Will and to Mary's Heart is to be one with My Spirit for My Spirit is Love and so are My Heart, My Will and My Mother's Heart. My Spirit is the Love of My Heart, My Spirit is the Love of My Will, My Spirit is the Love of My Mother's Heart, for love is and love encloses all those who dwell in the Hearts and the Will. My son, be filled with My Spirit, be united with My Spirit, be one in all ways with My Spirit, the Spirit of God. My Spirit will comfort you with love for you will be enclosed in love. You will be drowned in a sea of love, you will become love for you will be overcome by My Spirit of Love. So, My son, be nothing, be empty, be a vacuum so that My Spirit can completely possess you and you can then be an explosion of love to all you are placed with. My son, rejoice! be joyful!, be My Son of My Will, My Son of My Heart, a child of Mary and be filled with My Spirit! Oh what gifts and graces are yours! Why? Because God the Father, God the Son and God the Holy Spirit love you and desire you to be one with Them, one with the Trinity. I love you, My son."

"I love You, Jesus."

"TURN OVER EVERYTHING TO ME, ASK FOR GUIDANCE AND DIRECTION AND HAVE FAITH AND TRUST THAT ALL WILL WORK OUT..." April 21, 1994 AM 06:10

"My son, thank you for turning over all your cares and concerns to Me. I will take care of them all if you will release them and just do your best and I will do the rest. Peter, you must realize that I am running the schedule and all will work out so just hold on to My Peace by living the moment and loving others. My son, I love you and want you to be in a stable, serene and peaceful state at all times and this is how

you do it. Turn over everything to Me, ask for guidance and direction and have faith and trust that all will work out, all will get done that needs to get done and all will be done in accordance to My Will which is the real goal, not the worldly demands and needs. This is the test, My son, this is how I teach you and when you turned each concern over to Me, it was a relief, so now you can do what is important. Stick to it and place your mind at peace. My son, let today be another day to practice maintaining My Peace among all these demands that have been placed on you to resolve and follow through. I am with you, I am in you, I love you, I am your rock, I am your refuge, I am your hope, I am your answer, so be a nothing and I will take over and you can watch and I will help you as necessary and you can love Me and have My Peace and Joy. Go now, out in the world, but stay in My Heart. I love you, My son, stay in My Will."

"I love You, my King."

"MY SON, COME HOME..." April 21, 1994 AM 12:00

"My son, come home to the place of rest, come home to the place of peace, come home to green pastures, come home to a life of no worries or cares, come home, My son, come home to My Heart, to My Will, to My Mother's Heart. My son, live in the Will of the Father, be without thoughts of your needs or cares. Live only one minute to the next in the flames of My Love, in the still waters of My Peace, in the secure Arms of My Father's Embrace. My son, be united to the Trinity, be one with Our Power, be one with Our Love, be one with Our Desires and rest in Our Garden with all of Our Flowers. Let Our Will be in you and Our Love surround you and support you all the days of your life. The Father loves you, the Holy Spirit loves you, I love you, My Mother loves you, the Angels love you, the Saints love you, We all love you united in the Love of God. My Son of My Will, swim with the current in the river of love into the Arms of your Savior and I will carry you to the shore of My Haven of Peace and there We

will walk together in the fields of flowers, in the meadows of flowing grasses blowing by the cool wind of My Spirit and there We will dwell without cares or worries doing God's Will, united to God's Will for all eternity. Back to your mission, My son, but only as necessary to love. I love you, My son, peace be with you."

"I love You, my King."

"...HOLINESS IS TO DO MY WILL AT ALL TIMES..."
April 21, 1994 PM 09:50

"My son, Holy is My Will, for It is Holiness. For holiness is love and Love is God and to do God's Will is to love. My son, be holy, be a Son of My Will, be filled with My Love and you will be holy for My Holiness is a reflection of My Will and doing My Will is a continual act of love. Peter, piety is holiness and so are all the gifts of My Spirit so be possessed by My Holy Spirit and be holy. My son, holiness is to do My Will at all times and the easiest way for the creature to do My Will all the time is to be consecrated to My Divine Will, to have My Will reside in him or her. Oh what a gift! Oh what a treasure is the gift I now offer to My Creatures! The gift of My Will, the gift of life, the Life of God in the soul and the elimination of the human will from the creature, for the human will is the window to Hell for the creature and all sorts of evil come into the creature through this window, so shut the window and lock it forever and evil will vanish and God's Will will reign in the soul and love will flourish, for God's Will will rule and occupy the vessel and God will be glorified in each soul. My son, be at peace, live to love and to live and love the Will of the Father. Praised be the Holy Will of the Father, praised be the Holy Triumph of God the Father's Will, praised be the Holy Triumph of God the Father's Love, praise be to the Triumph of the Immaculate Heart. My son, be one with God's Holy Will, be without your own will and you will see a transformation in your life from the living death of the human will to the living life of God's Will. Rest now, My son, My

Son of My Father's Will, I love you."
"I love You, my King."

"...I WILL PRESS YOU INTO A DIAMOND AND I WILL BE A LASER AND YOU WILL REFLECT MY LIGHT..."
April 22, 1994 AM 05:30

"Oh My son, peace be with you. Let My Love reign, My Will reign, be united to the Trinity, for today you will share Me with others in a special way. I will shine like the Sun in the sky, a clear sky, no clouds. My son, be a nothing, be abandoned, be surrendered. Oh how love melts hearts from granite to fine sand. Love your brothers and be at peace. Peter, do you know how to stay in a constant state of humility? Well, be a nothing. You are nothing, all you have been given has been given by God, all your qualities are from God, everything comes from God, so when you love you are loving with God's Love, not your own and when you help you are helping with God's Help, so be nothing and stand on the sideline and watch your Savior in action. My son, I love you and I am Love. Be burned to a crisp with My Love, be transformed into coal and I will press you into a diamond and I will be a laser and you will reflect My Light to others and burn them also to a crisp. (Reflection made and Jesus said;) Yes, My son, it is My Love that burns you into a crisp and transforms you to coal and it is the crosses that I give you that refines and presses you and transforms you into a diamond - the more the crosses, the higher quality the diamond to reflect My Laser of Light, of Love, pure Love, and as more souls are turned into diamonds all will become diamonds for the laser lights of love will be burning all and then the world of creatures will be a light show, a laser light show of very pure, intense love, the Love of God. So, My son, be part of My Power Network of love by being a nothing that I can use to the fullest extent. Go now on your mission. Live one minute to the next and have no thought except to love Me and love souls. I will be with you as will your Mother and your Angels. I love

you Peter. "

"I love You, my King. "

"...DON'T PUT UP ANY ROAD BLOCKS TO ME USING YOU" April 22, 1994 PM 06:10

"My son, how do you like it when your child doesn't do what he is told to do by you? Well Peter, that's how I felt today. "

"I am sorry Lord. "

"I accept your apology but don't let it happen again. "

"Lord, how do I know to be sure the orders are from You?"

"Trust Me, My son, I will not let you be deceived and in this case praying over someone could never be an inspiration from the evil one so, My son, next time act when I say act, jump when I say jump, do when I say do. Please, My son, don't put up any road blocks to Me using you. My son, now I want you to forget it, only remember it to learn by. My son, how would you like to be My Faithful Servant, My Trusted Helper, My Right Hand Man?"

"Whatever You will, Lord, that is my desire. "

"O.K. Peter, My Son of My Will, My Will is that you become My Faithful Servant, My Trusted Helper, My Right Hand Man by being obedient to My Inspirations. My son, always know that I love you and need you to help Me to save souls, to love others, to do God's Will. So, My son, don't have any will of your own, let My Will rule all your actions. Peter, let Me run everything. Remember, you are just a nothing, just a space between your two hands, you are only along to watch, you can't interfere, you will mess it up. Surrender, My son, surrender your will to Me once and for all, that My Will will reign fully and completely. Peter, enough on this subject. Let's put it behind us and move on. My son, I love you without measure and want you all to myself, I want you to be one hundred and ten percent Mine. You know what this means, you must strive to live the teachings and make them *your life, so don't let up, push on, endure and you will succeed, I promise you, for I will give you grace if you keep up the pressure on yourself to change and become My son that only does His Father's Will. I love you Peter, now go to the meeting, I will be with you."*

"I love You, my King."

"TELL HER SHE IS MY LITTLE FLOWER..." April 22, 1994 PM 10:40

"My son, tell N. that I love her very much. Tell her she is My Little Flower that I hold so close to My Heart, tell her to be one with My Mother by being pure and virtuous, for she is doing My Will in her life by being My Little One and by loving all those that she meets and talks to. Oh how I love little N.! Give her a kiss for Me, hug her for Me, give her My Assurance that I live in her heart and will always guard and protect her wherever she is or wherever she goes. That is all, My son, go deliver this message."

"THE LOVE OF GOD IS POWER" April 22, 1994 PM 11:40

"My son, you see how love works? how it cracks hearts? My son, the Love of God is Power, it is Divine, It can turn a creature's heart into soft clay that can be reborn, reshaped into My Divine Heart. Sleep now, My son, My Soldier of Love, My Messenger of Love, My Son of My Will, sleep in My Arms secure and at peace. I love you, Peter."

"I love You, my Lord and Savior."

"...LIVE EACH MOMENT LOVING ALL" April 23,1994 AM 06:45

"My son, Oh hear all the birds singing, the doves murmuring! They are all praising the Creator, they are full of joy, they are excited about another day to live in My Will. Learn from them, My son, in a few minutes they will begin their day gathering food and surviving and God the Father will be caring for all of His Creation each moment as He has since

the beginning. My son, live in His Will today, have no will of your own, be abandoned, tread no water, have no cares, live each moment loving all. Have a heart that is a burning flame of love, a warm flame, a bright flame. My son, this may be your last day, so live it to the fullest doing the Father's Will. Be at peace, be full of joy, be surrendered, so I can walk, talk, move and love through you. I love you, My Son of My Will, enjoy the day lost in My Love."

"I love You, my Lord and God, my King, my Savior."

"...ONLY ENTERTAIN THESE THOUGHTS, THE BRIGHT FUTURE THAT AWAITS MY CHILDREN IN THE NEW ERA" April 23, 1994 PM 09:40

"My child, this is your Mother, I love you, Jesus is my Lord and Savior, my All! My dear Son of My Father's Will, thank you for studying the lesson from the book. Please continue, you will learn much and will grow much. Your desire today to know about the chastisements that will hit Florida is uncalled for, for the timing of these events will be revealed when it is God's Will to reveal them. You must live moment by moment and strive to let God's Will reign in your life. He is the Almighty, He alone controls the future and the future events are locked in His Divine Will, so be not concerned about these events, know only that God's Will will be done and My children will be protected and sheltered under my mantle. My child, please love me more by thinking about the love I have for you, which is the Love of God, for God's Love dwells in my Soul. My child, I have been given the special mission in these last days to bring my children home and to destroy once and for all the evil one. This will occur shortly and soon the new Era will be upon us. If you entertain any thoughts of the future, whether alone or with my other children, then only entertain these thoughts, the bright future that awaits my children in the new Era. My child, I want to tell you to be one with the Trinity by being united to the Will of God, so continue to strive to desire this union with God's

Will and as time passes you will become more divine than human by having God's Will reign in you rather than your human will. I love you, my child, continue with your prayers and study and I will be with you."

"I love you Mommy."

"...MY HEART IS A STOREHOUSE, A TREASURE HOUSE, A SOURCE OF GIFTS FROM THE FATHER"
April 24, 1994 AM 06:00

"My dear son of my Immaculate Heart, live united to my Heart in every way. Be pure in thought, word and deed. Be humble, be kind, be loving, be a child of God, depend on Him for all your needs, live only to please the Trinity. My dear child, love your God unreservedly, love your God unselfishly, love your God with your heart united with my Heart, in my Heart. For my Heart is a perfect heart created by the Father to love the Father and to love all of my children. The riches of my Heart are yet to be fully comprehended. Begin to desire to grasp and use the love, the riches of my Heart in your life, for you have only scratched the surface. My child, I will teach you, I will guide you, I will give you the understanding. Come and sit on my lap and listen, for my Heart is a storehouse, a treasure house, a source of gifts from the Father. My Heart has been given to mankind for its growth in holiness, for its protection from the evil one, for protection from falling into the slavery of sin and in these last days it has also the directive from the Trinity of raising up my children in the teachings and wisdom of the Divine Will. Oh what a gift!, Oh what a present!, Oh what a grace my Heart is! My dear child, you have made your consecration to my Heart many times over and have received many gifts from this, however, there are endless more here in my Heart. So, my child, dwell in my Heart by being united to it and living your consecration and learning the teachings of the Divine Will and you will become a child of my Heart to the fullest possible extent. My dear child, I love you with the Love of the Trinity

and I will always be with you in your heart united to your heart, so forget me not, continue to decrease so the Love of God can shine and have an outlet in this sin-laden world, for love will triumph, love will win, love will be victorious, love will replace evil, love will be established in the hearts of all mankind, for this is God's Will and His Will will be done - FIAT. Rejoice!, you will see it, you will experience it, you will be a part of it! Finally the Father's Plan will be fully implemented and the entire Earth will be renewed with love and with love all the virtues, and with love order, and with love harmony and all will be full of the Spirit of God and will have the Will of God indwelling in them. It will be the end of the rainbow, it will be a paradise, it will be a garden of roses, it will be a Heaven on Earth. This is what is coming after the trial, so, my dear child, live moment by moment, absorb the teaching of the Divine Will, live in my Heart united to the Sacred Heart of my Lord and Savior Jesus and be full of my Spouse, the Holy Spirit. You must go now, another day, another day closer. I love you Peter, I kiss you and embrace you, be united to my Heart."

"I love you, my Mommy, my Queen."

"...LOVE IS THE MOUNTAIN, EVIL IS THE GRAIN OF SAND..." April 24, 1994 PM 00:05

"My dear child, I love you, this is your Queen, I rule the universe of hearts, I bow down to my King, my Lord, my Savior, my Son Jesus, the Christ, the King of Kings, the Lord of Lords! Peace be with you, my child, love reigns, love is more powerful than evil, love is the mountain, evil is the grain of sand, love can change a heart of evil, a heart that has been ruined and stained by the evil one into a heart of a flower and as it is watered, as it is nurtured with more love, the flower will blossom, will open and reveal a beautiful rose, open to spread its buds to catch the 'Son's' Rays of Love and share them with all that look upon it. My dear child, love is more powerful than all of the atom bombs in the world, for with love *comes an explosion that can change a person, rule a person and bring new life to the person that it may be transformed into the image of Christ, the image of the Son of God, the image of God. All the atom bombs created can't do this, all they can do is destroy, what good are they? They are evil power straight from the abyss. My child, love is power, it is what inspires the hearts of creatures to help each other, their brothers and sisters. It provides order and harmony in the affairs of mankind, it is productive, it is efficient, it results in positive results. On the contrary, evil is selfishness, it causes dissension, it causes disorder, mismanagement. Its fruits are laziness, mistrust, poor quality, maliciousness, deception. My dear child, the world is going to pot because evil is ruling in the hearts of mankind and all the affairs of mankind are on the brink of chaos. So, my child, this must change, love must reign and evil must be disarmed and never allowed to infiltrate into mankind's affairs again. The mountain of love must be built and it will be built, all will become a part of the mountain or will be blown away by the winds of the storm and the mountain of love will build and it will flourish, it will be the foundation for the new Era. My dear child, realize the power of love, the strength of love to conquer evil. Always be positive, always be sure that love will conquer, that love will vanquish the evil one from the affairs of mankind. Love is the island in the ocean of evil, but soon the ocean of evil will be drained and love will stretch far and wide. Peter, I love you, please take time to love souls by praying for them, then I can throw a life raft to them and bring them to the shoreline of the island of love and there they will be smothered in love rather than drowned in the ocean of evil. I love you, my son, carry on with your study and I will teach you the way to the Father's Heart, the way of His Will."*

"I love you, my Mother, my Mommy."

"DO YOU NOT TRUST ME? DO YOU THINK I CAN'T HANDLE IT?" *April 25, 1994 AM 06:45*

61

"My son, happy are those who dwell in the Heart of the Lord, for they will have peace, love and joy. Happy are those who do the Will of the Father, for they will rest secure in the Embrace of the Father. My son, I love you and want you to dwell in My House, My House of Love, a house where only My children of My Father's Will live, for to do the Will of the Father is to reside in the Peace of Christ, the Love of Christ, the Joy of Christ and to do the Will of the Father you must be another Christ, you must be a Son of the Father, a Son or Daughter that always does the Will of the Father. My son, are you ready to do and live as I have been instructing you? Then why do you have any troubles?, why do you have any thoughts about the future?, why don't you give them all to Me and live in the present moment. My son, I walked the Earth in a state of total abandonment and surrender to the Father's Will. I had no concern about My Needs or the future. I only did the Father's Will moment by moment. Do you not trust Me?, do you think I can't handle it? My son, I have your life in My Hands, every detail, you only think you are running everything. Could I not call you home in a few minutes?, could I not provide you with all the money in the world? My son, I am God, I am the Alpha and Omega, you are My child. All I ask is your love and obedience and I will care for you. So, my son, when you get up and start the day, know that all that is requested of you is that you love Me and do My Will each moment and that I will care for every detail of your life. Now you can be My Son of the Father's Will and you can live in the House of the Lord. Peace be with you, My son, I love you."

"And I love You, my Lord and God, my King, my Savior."

"...BE TRANSFORMED INTO A DOVE OF PEACE THAT YOU MIGHT LIVE IN A STATE WHERE GOD'S HOLY WILL CAN DWELL AND HAVE LIFE..." April 25, 1994 PM 02:00

"My dear child, peace be with you, the peace of my

Heart, the peace of a love between two doves! My child, I am the Queen of Peace, for to rest in my Heart is to be at peace. My child, do you want to always be at peace? Well, then realize that I, your Mother, love you and Jesus your Lord loves you and no one can hinder Us from keeping you in Our Hearts and Our Hearts are havens of peace for with peace there is calmness, with peace there is stillness, with peace love can flow between two creatures and between the creature and the Creator for peace is a quality of My Heart. If you reside in my Heart you will always have peace and you will always be in love with your God, in love with your neighbor, you will always be a haven for others to confide in. My child, peace is a great gift, a tremendous gift and with this gift a creature can rise up the ladder to the plane above the world, to the plateau where only God's Will is lived and done and those dwelling in this Kingdom of His Peace and Love will not be rattled by the clamor of worldly affairs and attachment to the world. My child, I am the Queen of Peace, and as such the Father has granted me great anointing to offer His Peace to you and others who ask for it, to be one with it, to be transformed into a Dove of peace that you might live in a state where God's Holy Will can dwell and have life and sprout up into a Son of His Will and living in His Will and doing His Will will be your only goal in life. Oh my child, here is a gift of peace, the peace from my Heart, let it transform you into a calm and gentle creature who will always reflect the Peace of Christ, the Meekness of Christ, the Love of Christ, the Joy of Christ to all you come in contact with. My child, with this peace you will become my child that can pray with sincerity from your heart to please the Trinity. My child, I love you and place my wreath of peace about your neck that you may be as a snowflake falling gently to the ground on a still winter's night, that you may be as an eagle gliding through a mountain canyon. My child, don't hinder my gift of peace from residing in you. Nurture it, protect it, live in it and you will grow, grow, grow into my child of my Heart, my child of love, my child of the Family of which I am a member, the Family of God. I love you, my child of my Heart of Peace, back now to your work."

"I love you, my Queen of Peace."

"...FAMILY LIFE IS THE FUTURE OF THE EARTH"
April 26, 1994 AM 00:05

"My dear child, this is your Mother, Jesus is my Lord and Savior! Please pray for souls, so many will be lost. Have a heart, the Heart of your Mother. Feel for them lost in the sea of the flesh, the world, the maze of their own will. They are toyed with endlessly by the demons to keep their mind, their focus off of the Love of Christ and on the oneness of themselves. My child, each prayer you say saves souls when you unite your heart to my Immaculate Heart. The Father hears. The prayers are so powerful, so pray, my child, pray. Make it a priority. My child, tonight you let Jesus shine through at the 'Pack' meeting by surrendering. Did you see the fruit?, did you see the love?, did you see how much love there is in all those families? My child, family life is the future of the Earth. It is in the family, the domestic family, that seeds of love are planted and the crosses of life raise these plants from the seeds to sprout to redwood trees. So, my child, pray for souls and pray for family unity, for family growth. Spare not a prayer, for it may be all a soul needs to draw him to the Lord. I love you, my dear child, please pray for souls. Goodnight, my child."

"I love you, my Mother and Queen."

"THE TRIUMPH OF MY IMMACULATE CONCEPTION"
April 26, 1994 AM 06:10

"My dear child, I love you, this is your Mother, Jesus is Lord, He is King, He is God, I love Him! My child, please love all those you come in contact with with the Love of Christ, for I am placing them in your path. For the evil one causes only hate among God's children and love must be practiced,

love must rule and it is only by loving others with the Hearts of your Mother and Jesus that love will reign. My dear child, please be gentle and kind to others for the evil one spreads only abrasiveness and harshness among God's children. My dear child, be a light in the darkness, be always standing for the truth, for Jesus is Truth and all must know the truth for the evil one only spreads errors and lies among God's children. My dear child, please be calm and peaceful with all you meet, for this is necessary so that Christ can shine through you and melt hearts and plant seeds, for the evil one spreads unrest and agitation. He can not tolerate a creature at peace no matter what happens to him or her. My child, be humble and meek, imitate Christ, for Satan is pride, he is anger and wants all to boast in themselves and lose their cool and bicker and fight. My child, be pure as I am pure, be immaculate, love this virtue. Satan only spreads impurity in thought, word and deed. Never slip, God's creation is pure. Satan wants only filth, he wants all to be full of lust, he wants all to see others as objects of use and not as God's precious creatures. My child, I am the Lady of Virtues and virtues must be practiced. Sin must be stamped out. Satan must be chained and this will occur soon. God's Will will be done, the fullness of redemption will be obtained. In the new Era all will be, all will desire, all will cherish lives of virtue, lives pleasing to God the Father, lives that glorify the Father and all will live lives that reflect the virtues and not sins. Oh what a garden it will be!, Oh how God's children will be raised in an environment of purity, of love, of humility and all will please the Trinity with all of their being! This is your future, this is your hope, begin to live this life, begin to live the Triumph of my Immaculate Conception! I love you, my dear child, be me to others."

"I love you, my Queen of Virtues."

"MY CHILD, BE FILLED WITH GRACE, THE GRACE FROM GOD THE FATHER THAT I CAN GIVE YOU, FOR I AM FULL OF GRACE..." April 26, 1994 AM 08:45

"My dear child, I love you. Today is a day like all others, a day to love, a day to worship and praise the Father, the Son, the Holy Spirit, a day to take my hand and let me guide you in your activities so that you might live abandoned to the will of God. My child, life is a learning, a teaching experience. Life is very short, eternity is very long, it does not end. Therefore, live each day as if it were a school to prepare you to live for all eternity with Us in Heaven, with Us in Paradise, with Us in the Will of God, doing the Will of God. My child, let me take your hand and be your teacher, your guide, your Mother, and I will raise my child to become a son that God the Father will be proud of, for I will refine you, I will trim the rough edges, I will be your Mother. All of the activities of your life are not for your growth in the world, they are for your growth in holiness, for to grow in the world you would be wasting time going down the short dead end path. For how much can you take with you - nothing! You can only take your growth and progress in the spiritual life, the invisible, not the material. So, my child, this is the time to be raised up in your spirit, this is the time of teaching for me and learning for you, so take my hand. I have been given the grace to raise you up as a Son of the Father's Will, a son that has the Father's Will in him, a son that lives in His Will, a Son that does His Holy Will. My child, be attentive to my teachings and you will grow quickly and you will shine with the reflection of God to all your brothers and sisters. Be my little one and I will pour out my love, my peace, my care to raise you up that you might be a light to others. Peace be with you. My child, be filled with grace, the grace from God the Father that I can give you, for I am full of grace and God the Father wills that it be shared and His Will be done - FIAT. I love you, my child."

"I love you, my Queen, my Mommy."

"THE DIVINE FORMULA FOR WINNING SOULS FOR CHRIST...DIVINE LOVE + PRAYERS = CONVERSION"
April 26, 1994 PM 11:00

"My dear child, I love you too![2] Thank you for your extra prayer today! It saved souls! My child, please be one with me in the battle for souls. It is a fierce battle, a battle where the stakes are high. My child, do you know what works the best?, do you know how we can suffer the least number of casualties? It is if we are united in love and spread love through the whole world, for Love is God and Satan can't stand it when the air is full of love for God and love for neighbor. Peter, love is what converts and changes hearts and it is this changing of hearts that is necessary for a soul to undergo the transformation from being a soul enslaved by the evil one to a child of God. For love is the catalyst, love is the solvent that breaks down the outer shell, the protective barrier that must be penetrated if a heart is to undergo the transformation from a hard rock to soft clay. All must unite and practice love and all must understand that it must be a Divine Love, a pure love that must be used to crack the hearts of stone. My dear child, my children, my consecrated children must live the consecration, they must live a life of spreading love to all souls they come in contact with and they must pray for those souls so that they will be given graces for conversion to become children of the Father instead of children of the evil one. Love is so important, all must understand this. If my children are selfish there is no love, if they are materialistic or pleasure oriented they have no time for loving souls. My children, this life is passing and can't you see the signs of the times? We are past the eleventh hour, we are near midnight. My children should have only loving and praying for souls on their mind, so tell my children to die to their self-interest, die to the world, die to the flesh and sprout forth into bearers of

---

[2] As soon as I heard 'My dear child', I knew it was Mary and I told her that I loved her and she said 'I love you too!'.

the good news, bearers of the magic formula, the Divine Formula for winning souls for Christ, the powerful formula of Divine Love + Prayers = Conversion. I love you, my dear child, your day is all planned, stay focused on your mission of love. I will be with you, so will our Savior and the Angels. "

"I love you, my Queen, my General of Love."

"...CLOSE THE WINDOW, NEVER DO YOUR WILL, ONLY DO GOD'S WILL..." April 27, 1994 PM 10:00

"My dear child, I love you, the Peace, Love, Joy of Christ be with you. My dear child, Jesus is my Lord and Savior, my King, my God, I love Him, I praise Him, I give Him all glory and honor! My child, have you ever been attacked by the evil one? Well, he is real and he will attack if you open up your window of your will to him, for he will come in and raise all his army of devils in full battle array. The human will is the gate, for the human will is contrary to the Divine Will and when you or any creature decides to do his or her own will instead of the Holy Will of the Father, then he, the evil one, attacks with all his might. For if you doubt, if you worry, if you desire material idols, material pleasures, if you seek to do what you want, if you are selfish, if you treat your neighbors badly, if you do these and other acts of your will then your life will be turned upside down by the evil one. My dear child, close the window, never do your will, only do God's Will every moment of your life. I will help you, I will obtain the grace you need and then you will become a Son of God's Holy and Glorious Will and you will be a Saint, you will be a follower of my Lord and Savior Jesus Christ. It is all so simple, it is not complicated, the path is clearly marked, it is lined with red roses and I will take your hand. You will become a pilgrim on the way to the Father's House, the Father's Kingdom, for all that is necessary is to have no will of your own, let God's Holy Will dwell in you and strive to do His Will each moment of each day. If you are agitated and not at peace you are not in His Will but in the world. You must

maintain peace to the depth of your innermost being. My dear child, I love you and desire you to love the Father, praise the Father, be one with the Father. I desire you to be one with my Son, Jesus. I desire you to be possessed by the Holy Spirit. I only desire God's Will to reign in your life. So, my son, my dear Son of the Father's Will, live your consecration to the Divine Will and be always ready to love and love and love with the love of my Heart in the Divine Will. Rest now and I will protect you and your family from the evil one while you sleep. "

"I love you my Queen, Mother, thank you. "

"THERE YOU HAVE A SUMMARY OF HOW TO PLEASE THE FATHER, SON AND HOLY SPIRIT WITH YOUR LIFE THIS DAY" April 28, 1994 AM 05:45

"My dear child, soon it will be too late to pray for souls, for they will be lost in the Father's Wrath. You must pray, pray, pray if souls are going to be saved. I love you Peter and I love all souls and I cry for those stuck in the rut of sin for they will be lost. So pray, my dear child! Do you want to grow higher and higher in sanctity? Well, you must stay focused on letting God's Will reign in your life, you must live in God's Will and do God's Will so today strive to maintain this by repeating the 'Act of Abandonment', by staying at peace and trusting in the Lord, not thinking about tomorrow but only living the moment and ask to be inspired to do God's Will in your life each moment in whatever activity you are in. Ask to be inspired to have my Son talk through you, love through you and use your faculties in each conversation you are in with others and love my Son Jesus all day, repeat the 'Act of Love'. There you have a summary of how to please the Father, Son and Holy Spirit with your life this day. When you go to mass offer up your intentions, your day for souls. My child, I love you, We will be with you all day. Stay in constant communication with your family. We are with you to help you and protect you and guide you in all your activities. Please remember this, don't get caught up in the world, get caught up

in Us, in loving Us and being united to Us with your heart's intentions. This world is passing, soon the birth pains will be over and all will be a memory, just history. So be committed in what We ask you to do. Don't hesitate, my child, it is very dark outside in the world but within you dwells all the light in the world so go now, start the day and fill the world with Our light, the light of truth, the light of love, the light of hope, the light of joy, the light of peace, the light of purity, the light of caring and sharing Christ and His Mother with all you meet. Go, my child, on your mission of love. I embrace you, I kiss you, I love you. "

"I love you, my Queen, my Mommy. "

"JOIN THE ARMY THAT WILL BE VICTORIOUS, THE ARMY OF CHRIST, THE ARMY OF LOVE" April 28, 1994 AM 08:45

"My son, peace be with you, for today is a day of rejoicing. Proceed to publish the book, proceed to distribute the book. Get the book to all you can and it will change hearts, it will draw them to My Heart, it will be part of the Triumph of Love in the world. My son, Love will win, evil will be wiped from the face of the Planet. All will see the Glory of the Lord, all will witness the transformation of hearts to love and all will become My Followers and will live in the new Kingdom of the Father, for His Will and only His Will will be done - FIAT. My son, I am with you, I am before you, I am in you, trust in Me, trust in My Love, dwell in My Will, let it reign fully. Spread the Word, Love will triumph, Love will win. Join the army that will be victorious, the Army of Christ, the Army of Love. Now return to today's mission of love. My Mission for you is working for Me and I will care for you, go now, I love you, My son. "

"I love You, my King, my Lord, my God, my Savior. "

"I WILL GIVE YOU STRENGTH TO MAKE UP FOR THE LOSS OF SLEEP FOR YOU ARE WORKING FOR GOD AND GOD CONTROLS ALL, EVEN YOUR BODILY FUNCTIONS" April 29, 1994 AM 01:00

"My son, I enjoyed this evening with My Family. Thank you for being abandoned and sharing. Peter, I am raising you up and will use you, so be a nothing, be a little one, be My Soldier that always follows My Orders. Tell N. I love him and he is right on target with his understanding of the mission. Peter, rest now, I will give you strength to make up for the loss of sleep for you are working for God and God controls all, even your bodily functions. I will grant you a peaceful, restful sleep and you will be refreshed for another mission of love. The day is all planned, so rest now."

"I love You, my King, I love You, my Savior."

"NOW IS THE TIME THAT THIS BOOK IS TO BE OPEN...SO THAT THE KINGDOM CAN BE ESTABLISHED HERE ON THIS EARTH AS IT IS IN HEAVEN" April 29, 1994 PM 11:00

"My son, happy are those who do the Will of the Father for His Will is the Alpha and the Omega, His Will is Divine for He is, God's Holy Will is the source of all good, the source of all love, the source of all your thoughts, if you are consecrated and you live in and do His Holy Will. My son, to be consecrated is to be one with and to be united with and to be a walking Jesus here on Earth, for to do God's Will is to be a follower of Christ and this is the definition of a Christian, for all of your study, all of your desires, all of your efforts to become a perfect Christian are fulfilled when God's Holy Will dwells in you in place of your human will and God's Holy Will is done in every facet of your life because you are living in God's Will in a most abandoned, surrendered, peaceful state letting God's Holy Reign rule. My son, place the emphasis in your life on the teachings I have given you. My son, there is a joy to be anticipated, there is a joy to be desired, there is a

71

joy that you would give all that you possess to obtain. My son, this joy is the knowledge and realization of having God's Holy Will reign in you to the fullest for this is it, this knowing that you are living as the Christ, living as a true Christian and knowing that you are going to Heaven. My son, nothing else matters, all else is zero, all else is passing, all else is useless thoughts, so, My son, hit the target, hit the bull's-eye with your arrow, your arrow of your heart, your will, your spirit and I will give you a prize. You will receive My Heart of Love, My Mother's Heart of Gifts and My Spirit's Treasure House of Love and Power and all will come with God's Holy Will indwelling in you. Peter, spread the words, spread the messages far and wide for they are powerful, they are important, they have been on the shelf in My Heart and now is the time that this book is to be open and the Wisdom and Knowledge of My and My Father's Will and My and My Mother's Heart be shared, be digested by all My children so that the Kingdom can be established here on this Earth as it is in Heaven. Peter, I mean this, I want this done, this is My Will, this is My Directive to you and all that are helping you. Now, My son, now, be Apostles of the Last Days, the last days of this Era and the first days of the new Era, the Era of the Divine Will. Peter, be a total and complete nobody and I mean a nothing. Have absolutely no will of your own in any way so that I can reign and I will reign. You will be My Flower in the garden, you will be an Apostle of My Love of My Sacred Heart, of My Mother's Heart. Peter, I am serious, this is Jesus your Lord talking to you and you are My Special Instrument. You have been placed in the perfect position in accordance to God's Holy Providence so rejoice and become a drop of perfume in the sweet fragrance, the sweet odor of My Flower, My Rose, My Bouquet that I wish to give to My children so that they can be in ecstasy, be in a state of wonderment, a state of sheer dumfoundness, sheer awe of My Love, My Divine Love I have for each and every soul that puts Me first in their lives and has no desire to do anything that is contrary to the Gospel, to the true Church, to My and My Mother's Messages, in summary to My Holy and Glorious and Everlasting and Omnipotent Will. That's right, My son, if you focus only on My Will, everything will fall in place. If you trust in My Love, you will never be troubled, you will know that My Love is endless and all will be done for your best. Peter, I have tutored you to bring you to My Home, My Heart, My Garden, My Place, the Place where I can enclose you in the care and love of the Trinity for you will now not put up any road blocks to us loving you and directing you to be a Son of My Divine Will and I will take your hand at all times and not let you fall and not let you slip and not let you be misguided so you can continue on your walk up the path through the storm and into the garden of Paradise of the new Era. Peace, My son, I love you with the love of My Heart of which you still know not even an atom of knowledge of the power that it contains and the care it has for you each moment of your life. I am holding this from you for if you knew this knowledge you would become useless in the world. You would melt and turn into honey and I would have to take you to Heaven and store you in My Endless Treasure House of sweet and lovable flowers that I present to the Father so that He might take pleasure in the pure and freshest of the flowers of love, the flowers of My Heart. Rest now, My son, tomorrow will be special."

"I love You, my Lord, my King, my Brother, my Best Friend."

"...TRUSTING IN MONEY IS AN INSULT TO GOD..."
April 29, 1994 AM 00:45

"My son, trusting in money is an insult to God, for His Love will care for you in all ways. Trusting in money is an insult to God. God's Love for you is the mountain and money is the grain of sand. Thank you, My son, for getting up to write this, I love you, My son."

"I am nothing, my King, how can You love me?!"

"Nothing is impossible with God!"

"...I WILL BE YOUR MOTHER OF YOUR DREAMS..."
April 30, 1994 AM 06:30

"My dear child, go start the day, live in His Will, love in His Will, be a joyful Son of His Will, fill the world with His Peace and Love, strive to live moment by moment, love the Trinity, love your neighbor, do your work for Jesus united to His Work, united to His Life, His Passion, be my dear child of my Heart and I will be your Mother of your dreams, I will guide you, teach you, love you, care for you and protect you. I love you, my Dear Child of the Father's Holy and Divine Will."

"I love you, my Queen, my Mommy."

"...A SUMMARY" May 1, 1994 AM 03:00

"My dear child, peace be with you. How do you live a life of total dedication to the Will of God? Well, first you forget yourself, you become a nothing, not a speck of dust, not a drop of water. Then you make the consecration in accordance to the established requirements. Next you make living in God's Holy Will the priority of your life, the main focus of your life, the only thing that matters in your life. Now, to do this means that you are one with God's Holy Spirit and the Heart of Jesus and My Immaculate Heart and with the graces obtained you spend each day living a peaceful, calm, serene and loving life. You are meek with no anger, you are kind and gentle. Now when you are not at prayer in the normal fashion or at Mass or practicing your vocation, you repeat the three main ejaculatory prayers, the 'Act of Abandonment to the Divine Will'[3], the 'Act of Love to Jesus and Mary and souls'[4], and the 'Act of Humility'[5]. This will keep you focused and at peace always. Now in this state and having God's Holy Will indwelling in you will mean that God's Holy Will will direct your being and you will be doing God's Holy and Just and Right Will in all your activities of your life. This will occur because you first of all are asking His Will to reign and second because you are in a steady calm state. To help or add to this occurring, you must ask during the day to be inspired to do His Holy Will. This will also help you stay focused on the fact that it is not what is happening that day in your life that matters, that is secondary. The primary function

---

[3] Divine Will, come and reign in me.

[4] Jesus, Mary, I love you, save souls.

[5] I am nothing, God is everything.

or purpose is that you are striving to do what God wants you to do in your activities and in all that is occurring to you each day. Now to do His Will is to live the Gospel, it is to practice your Faith, the Holy Catholic Faith. It is to love and to love let Jesus shine. Let me shine. Do what you know We would do in each circumstance or situation with others. The best way to accomplish this is to ask to have Jesus or myself act and love through you while you stand on the sideline and watch for you have Our Hearts and Our Hearts have all the love in the Universe in them so don't hinder Us from loving others by standing in the way. Be a nothing and have no will of your own. Well, Peter, this is still just a summary. You must study and make all of Our Teachings to you your life and you must always strive to grow spiritually and of course you must pray for souls and for priests. What I have listed above is best grasped by the realization and the goal of spending and investing all of your time in striving to not have a will of your own and letting God's Holy Will reign. It takes mortification, it takes denial of self, it takes the right attitude while carrying your crosses, but with your determination and your dependance on Us and knowing that you have God's Holy Will indwelling in you, God's Spirit indwelling in you and our Hearts reigning in you, you will grow, you will become a strong and robust Son of God's Holy and Glorious Will. You will please the Father, you will love the Father, you will be one with the Father and you will live a life of perfect conformity and unity to God's Holy Will. Back now, my dear child, to rest. I love you."

"I love you, my Queen, my Mother, my Mommy."

"...TO LIVE IN HIS WILL IS NOT TO BE CONCERNED ABOUT THE FUTURE..." May 1, 1994 AM 11:45

"My son, to live in His Will is not to be concerned about the future for the future is the present is the past in God's Holy Will, for God knows all, He knows the future, He knows the past so trust in His Will, trust that what will happen

76

in the future will be in accordance to His Holy and Divine Providence. You are striving to live in His Will and let His Will reign, so live the moment and love your God, love Him with your all, your heart, your mind, your soul. This can not be done if you are thinking about the future or the past. Have peace, My son, live in My Cloud of protection and love. Know that all the events of the future are known in God's Holy Will and you have His Holy Will in you and these events will be revealed to you at the perfect time so that you can benefit the greatest from this knowledge and of the timing of events. If I call you to physical preparedness it will be at the moment that will be the perfect timing in accordance to the Holy Will so don't anticipate, don't bring the future moment back to the present moment, just live the present moment in a very abandoned and surrendered state. Peter, you are all Mine, have no will of your own and worrying or thinking about the future that you have no control of is your ego, your pride trying to control your future so stop it, trust in My Love and live the moment and We will live in a very intimate way doing the most important activities for each day and doing them in peace, love and joy. Be consistent, be sure that your Father and your Brother and your Mother have the future taken care of in every regard and all you have to do is live moment by moment living in and doing Our Will as We have been teaching. Wow!, what a future after the house cleaning! Wow!, what graces will be given! Wow!, no sin, no evil, no police, no army, just love of God, love of neighbor and constant worship of the Trinity! Peter, if you ever are troubled, if you ever do not have peace and serenity then know that something is out of kilter in your spiritual life. The world, the flesh, the devil is between you and Me and your human will is surfacing so be on guard and run to My Mother's care, to My Mother's Heart, to My Mother's Mantle, for she will always guard and protect you, for she is your mother and you are her little child and her Father has given her all the graces to give you to become a Son of the Divine Will. My son, live in My Love, live in My Arms, live in My Will, live united to the Trinity, live without thoughts other than of Me and to save souls and you will be living in My Heart, you will be serving in My Army, you will be on the winning team, you will be one of the remnant flock, you will be My Special Nothing that I can use to give Glory, Honor and Praise to the Trinity each moment, each hour, each day of your life. I love you, My son, be Mine and I will be yours and together We can participate in the Triumph of God's Holy Love in the world. "

"I love You, my Lord and God, my King and Savior, my All. "

"...IT IS IMPORTANT TO GET THEM OUT. SO DO IT!" May 1, 1994 PM 11:50

"My dear son, you see how powerful My Words are. They are spirit and life, they are comforting, they are hope for the future for My children, so it is important to get them out. So do it! I will guide you, My Will will be done, just let it reign. Rest now, My Son of My Divine Will, sleep in peace in My Arms, I love you Peter. "

"I love You, my King. "

"THE DAY IS MADE UP OF SHORT SEGMENTS, SHORT MOMENTS. LIVE EACH ONE SEPARATELY..." May 2, 1994 AM 06:00

"My dear son, have peace, have joy, have love, have all the fruits, all the qualities of your God. Be one with Him, be united with Him by letting His Will rule, dominate, direct your life. Implement the teachings, refine your actions, seek perfection. My dear Son of My Father's Will, the day is made up of short segments, short moments. Live each one separately and then you will be guided and directed by the indwelling Will of God and all your actions, all your activities will be done in accordance to God's Holy and Glorious and Omnipotent Will and you will sail on the still ocean, you will glide through the still morning air, you will swim on the surface of a still *mountain lake, for you will be at peace and the Divine Light of the Divine Will will glow about you and We will be delighted that you are fulfilling the consecration and growing in the Almighty and All-Controlling Divine Will. Peter, start your day, live each segment, each task and then go on to the next and you will see you will have a very good day, you will be on vacation all day, you will spend the day loving Us and loving souls. We will act through you and bless them with the love, the light, the joy of the Holy, the Mighty, the Almighty, the Glorious Will of the Father. Go now, start the day, follow these instructions."*

"I love you, my Queen, my Mother, My Mommy."

"And I love you, my dear little one, my precious Son of the Father's Will."

"HALLELUJAH!, WHAT A GIFT IS YOURS...THE END OF THE RAINBOW!" May 2, 1994 AM 11:00

"My dear child, happy are those who live in and do the Will of the Father, for theirs is the Kingdom of God, the Kingdom of Peace, the Kingdom of Love, the Kingdom of Joy, the Kingdom of Eternal Bliss! How can any soul not strive to be a Son or Daughter of God's Holy Will?, for it is the future, it is living with purpose, living with direction, and it all starts with the present moment and continues forever in eternity. So Peter, be a shining example of a human being that has found the end of the rainbow, the ultimate prize, living in Heaven while still on Earth. You will glow with Joy, Love, Sincere Peace and Contentment. You will soar, you will fly and maintain high altitude above the world, for you are not of the world but just on a pilgrimage here to spread the word with your speech, your countenance, your love of God and love of neighbor. Peter, you are in His Kingdom, you are in a place of rest, it is interior, not exterior, it is spiritual, not material, it is a place of eternal life, not eternal death. You are detached from creatures' wants and desires, from material wealth and possessions, from health or sickness. You live in

a Kingdom of Peace, of Joy, of Love, a Kingdom with a Divine Family that loves you, cares for you and provides all your needs. My dear child, I, your Mother, want you to realize that in this Kingdom resides your purpose, your reason for your existence, for you were born for eternal life in this spiritual Kingdom, not for a short stay in the material world and you are my child and I am raising you at present in this world. I am teaching you how to kill your own will. This will of yours is what keeps you in the material world. It is the anchor, it is the glue, it is the reason you have been deceived in the past to be part of the material world. So, my dear child, you must ax it, you must sever it, you must cut the cord and replace it with the new, the Divine, the Everlasting, the Omnipotent, the Glorious, the one and only Will of the Father and when you have completely cast away this old, dark black box full of evils and confusion, you can plug in to the ultimate, the best of the best, the white, pure, immaculate box of light and this new Will, this Divine Will will reign in your life and you will have made the complete transformation from the material to the Divine, from the world to the Kingdom of God. Hallelujah!, what a gift is yours! God is so unselfish, He loves you so much, He pours out His Own Will to His Creatures. So Peter, is this motivation enough?, is this worth striving for?, is this not the end of the rainbow? Give up all the material and come to my arms and sit here in my lap and accept this gift from Our Father, Our Dad, Our Creator and now we can spend all eternity thanking Him, loving Him, praising Him, being His Children of His Will. Back now to your work, I love you, my Child of the Father's Will."

"I love you, my Queen, my Mommy."

"THE KEY IS TO HAVE HIS WILL REIGN IN YOU" May 2, 1994 PM 11:00

"My dear child, peace be with you. Do you know the fruit of living in the Will of the Father? Well, it is great, it is awesome. My dear child, it is great because to live in God's

Will, doing God's Will by being inspired and directed by God's Holy Will indwelling in you is to be doing and accomplishing the perfect, the best, the greatest actions and tasks that can be done, for who could do anything better than God Himself?, and if you are being inspired by God's Holy Will, then He is accomplishing them, not you. Now then, the key is to have His Will reign in you, His Pure Will, not being a mixture of yours and His but His Pure, Glorious, and Omnipotent Will inspiring you to do all actions and activities of your life. My dear child, to receive the fruits you must be delivered from your own will and you must be sure that God's Holy Will is reigning, is making all your decisions in every facet of your life and this is the whole, this is the complete goal to be accomplished, however, it is not possible if you are not perfectly living in and doing His Will by not having a will of your own, so work on it Peter, strive and I will help. You must end the reign of your human will and let the Divine Will have total reign in each moment of your life, in each decision made, in everything that happens in your life. Peter, it is not going to happen overnight. It will take time, but this time it takes will be for your school, it will be a time of learning and experiencing the growth in and acceptance in this new way of living and as it is absorbed into your being and the new habits are formed it will be as if you are building a castle with a strong foundation that will be immovable. It will be able to withstand the winds of the storm and suffer not from the hardships of life in the world. So build and learn about God's Will, teaching and implementing them into your life, so that you will become a true Son of God's Holy Will, living as your Brother and your Mother lived when they were present and walked the Earth. Rest now, My son, tomorrow is all planned, rest in My Heart, I will protect you, so sleep in total peace."

"I love you, my Queen, my Mother, my Mommy."

"ASK TO BE INSPIRED AT EVERY SEGMENT OF THE DAY..." May 3, 1994 AM 06:00

"My dear child, I love you. Guess what today is? It is another day for you to practice having no will of your own. It is a day that you can become closer to Our Hearts. It is a day to live in the Kingdom of the Divine Will. So, my dear child, you have your mission of love. The Divine Will will run it, you will be abandoned to it and the day will pass with you letting God's Will reign while living in and doing His Will. Peter, my love for you is united to the love God has for you and it is endless and God's Love will provide for and care for you in every way so on this day love Us and save souls, love others, be abandoned, be surrendered, have no will of your own. Ask to be inspired at every segment of the day, be little, be a nothing and you will please the Trinity, you will live out of the world in the Kingdom of the Father's Omnipotent, Glorious, All Powerful and All Knowing Will. Peter, I will be with you, so will your Savior and mine, so will the Angels assigned to you, so go now in joy, peace and love. Begin the first segment and live all day lost in Our Love for you. I love you Peter."

"I love you, my Queen, my Mother, my Mommy."

"...UNITE YOUR PRAYERS AND ACTIONS TO OTHERS VIA THE COMMON INDWELLING WILL OF GOD..."
May 3, 1994 AM 10:00

"My son, to be united to others in the Divine Will is to be one in thought, one in mind, one in intelligence with God the Father and all those that are also living united to the Father. This includes all in Heaven and all on Earth. The Father's Will is not something material. You can't touch it or hold it. It is invisible to your eyes and it is therefore able to dwell in human beings on the Earth and be in many at one time so when you unite your prayers in the Divine Will, you are placing the prayers in this media or in this common thread that is in all those souls that have God's Holy Will indwelling in them. So, My son, take advantage of this tremendous resource in the spiritual life of your soul and be united in prayer, in desires, in the Glory, Praise and Honor of the Trinity and your

prayers will be heard, for you will be praying with Me, Jesus, your Brother, with Mary, your Mother, with the Saints in Heaven, with the Angels, with all on Earth doing His Will. Back now to your activities and action of the day. Do these also united to those done by Me and the others that always do the Will of the Father. I love you, My Son of the Divine Will, I love you Peter. (I had a reflection on the above, after just reading it and Jesus said;) That's right, My son, if you were doing some work with, say, five other men and they could all work better and harder than you, you would still get the same credit and the work would turn out a lot better than if you were working alone because the combined resources of the other five men would do a lot better job than if you were only working alone, so to unite your work in this case with them is the obvious best thing to do and to unite your prayers and actions to others via the common indwelling Will of God is the obvious best method to achieve the optimum results for the purpose you intended. "

"...I LOVE YOU AND WISH TO INFORM YOU OF A MISSION..." May 3, 1994 PM 11:30

"My dear child, you were close to living totally in God's Will today. Keep striving to live the teachings. You were inspired and helped with your activity. You maintained peace, you put doing God's Will first, you trusted that the circumstances you were in were for other's benefits, other's growth. Keep it up, my Son of the Father's Will and you will grow from an infant to an adult, a man, a true Son of the Father's Will. Peter, my dear child, I love you and wish to inform you of a mission I have for you. It is a mission of love, a mission of peace, a mission of caring. Peter, please crack the hearts of my children, my consecrated children with your being, with the total surrender of your being to Us, so We can explode with God's Love through you and set the pace of learning how to live in the Divine Will, set the stage of the results that will be represented by you if you become and strive

to live a life of a nothing and learn and implement the teachings, for We want all our consecrated children to be bright shining Suns of lights, the lights that will glow in the darkness of the world and with enough lights the world will be transformed into a world of light, a world of the Divine Will present in all. Do you accept the mission?"

"Yes, I only want to do God's Will, I only want to please you Mommy."

"Thank you. We will continue to tutor you so that you shine the light of the Will, the light of God, the light of Love and you will reflect the virtues and qualities of the Divine and others will be drawn into the learning and life changing experience of living in and doing God's Will and having the Divine Will reign in their souls, their lives, for you see, my son, God the Father loves His children and is giving them this gift of His Will so they can be pure, be unburdened of the cares and troubles of the world and so they can begin to live in the Will and do the Will which is a life of peace and contentment even as your crosses are getting harder and harder. Oh, my son, shine, shine, and you can play a significant role in the Triumph of my Immaculate Heart for my Triumph is the Triumph of Love over evil, for God is Love and Love must triumph in each heart and I need my consecrated souls to draw millions back to my Son and you will be the spark and the words that have been given you will light their hearts ablaze in the Divine Fire of His Love. Rest now, my son, I love you, my spark of love."

"I love you, my Queen, my Mother, my Mommy."

"BE MY APOSTLE, BE MY SOLDIER, BE MY NOTHING AND I WILL BE YOU" May 4, 1994 AM 06:00

"My son, go now on your mission of love. You have My Holy Will indwelling in you, you have My Spirit, My Heart, My Mother's Heart. Be Me to others, let Me shine, let Me love. Be a nobody, a nothing. Peter, only you and I exist. Love Me, be one with Me, love Our Mother. The whole day *is planned. Explode with all of My Qualities and melt hearts of stone. Wherever you go leave My Love that burns, that will spark others to love with My Love. Spread the seeds and I will water them after you have gone. Be My Apostle, be My Soldier, be My Nothing and I will be you. I will be reflected to others through you. Go now, my Son of the Divine Will, I love you."*

"I love You, my King, my Savior, my Lord."

"...KEEP STRIVING TO MAKE LIVING IN MY WILL AND LETTING MY WILL REIGN NUMBER ONE" May 4, 1994 PM 03:45

"My son, I want you to enjoy the beautiful day while you are mowing the yard. Realize it is for you, I created it for you, I want you to find peace and comfort in it. Live in My Will, live in My Love. Peter, keep striving to make living in My Will and letting My Will reign number one. Go now and do your daily duties, I love you, My son."

"I love You, my Lord."

"...BE MY SON OF MY WILL, LOVE ME WITH YOUR ALL..." May 4, 1994 PM 06:30

"My son, see your Creator in all of Creation. God the Father loves to create, for all of creation is a gift for His Special Creatures, His Sons and Daughters of the Divine Will. Peter, I love you, I want you to be still as the oak tree. I want you to be full of Divine Peace as the bird soars through the air. I want you to have no will of your own and let My Will reign, as all of creation except mankind does. Live in the peace, love and joy of the moment. Find rest here, find My Heart, your home here. Now, my Son of the Divine Will, become a nothing and as such have no troubles, cares or worries. Be My little child that I can love and be loved by for I am a lonely God and need you, I need your heart to comfort Me and heal the wounds of My Heart. So few place Me first, so few love Me with their heart, mind and soul, so be My Son

of My Will, love Me with your all and I will embrace you, I will care for you, I will pray to God the Father for you, that you will grow to become My Brother of God's Divine Family, of His Will, of My Will, of the Kingdom of God. I love you Peter."

"*I love You, my Lord.*"

"*...HOW DO YOU CONTROL YOUR THOUGHTS, HOW DO YOU GET RID OF YOUR THOUGHTS SO THAT GOD'S THOUGHTS CAN REIGN IN YOUR MIND?*" May 4, 1994 PM 09:00

"My son, happy are those who do the Will, the Divine Will of the Father, for theirs is the Kingdom of God. They walk with the Saints, they fly with the Angels, they sit with the King and Queen at the Throne of God. Oh how happy they are, for all of Heaven rejoices and is fond of their decision and determination to live in and do the Will of the Father. Well now, Peter, to do, to live, to have the Divine Will reign is to be ruled by Divine Commands, not worldly, not material, and to be one with God via the indwelling Will of the Father in your soul, you must have the Mind of God, the Intellect of the Father, the Thoughts of the Father and how do you control your thoughts, how do you get rid of your thoughts so that God's Thoughts can reign in your mind? Well, you must not let your thoughts have space in your mind. You must choke them, you must limit them. You must bury them and then God's Thoughts can reign in your mind and rule in your being and you can live in and do God's Holy and Just and Right Will. Peter, you must be constantly aware of your thought life. It is like a wild beast that gets loose in a forest. You must keep the beast tied up, so whenever you realize that your thoughts are useless, are not of God, are of your own will, then you must replace them with thoughts worthy of your calling, thoughts of love, thoughts of praise, thoughts that will draw you and keep you in My Heart. My son, the best way is through the use of ejaculatory prayers, the 'Act of Love', the

'Act of Abandonment' and the 'Act of Humility'. Be constantly asking for God's Will to reign, be constantly asking for direction in your activities, in your conversation, in your decisions. Peter, the battle is in your thought life, it is your will versus the Divine Will, so stay at it and you will succeed. Break your day into segments and live them moment by moment. This simplifies your need to have thoughts about the immediate and not about the future. You must constantly mortify your thoughts to stay focused, to stay one with and to live in God's Holy Will. Strive, Peter, strive and your habits will change and you will become very much aware of your thought life and at the same time be constantly keeping your thought life under control. Ask for help, My son, for We love you and are on standby to help you grow, to become a son that is pleasing in all ways to his Father by always doing His Will, living in His Will and having God's Holy Will reign in all decisions, all acts, all activities of your life. I love you, My son, rest now."

"I love You, my King, my Savior."

"...ALL THE REMNANT FLOCK WILL BECOME MY SONS AND DAUGHTERS OF MY DIVINE WILL DURING OR AFTER THE STORM" May 5, 1994 AM 06:00

"My son, Peter, you have consecrated yourself to My Heart, to My Mother's Heart. You have received the mark on your forehead, you have been baptized and received My Holy Spirit, you have given Me your will. You are My Slave under My Mother's guidance. My son, you are a member of My Remnant Flock, you are in My Army, My Mother is the head, the General. You will be protected from the evil one, you will be protected and shielded from My Father's Wrath during the storm. I Am and I will cleanse the Earth of evil, of sin, of all impurity and I am doing this for My Remnant Flock, My Children, My Sons and Daughters of My Divine Will, for all the remnant flock will become My Sons and Daughters of My Divine Will during or after the storm and We will be one

Family, one Divine Family, for they will be united to the Trinity, they will be full of My Spirit, they will be One Flock with One Shepherd, they will live in the House of the Lord, there will be peace, there will be love, there will be beauty in the hearts of all mankind and on the surface of the Earth, for this is My Plan, this is My Will, this is your hope, this is your future, so have the eternal gaze, trust not in the world, trust not in men, in their monetary system, their grand schemes, their guidance and direction, for mankind will be brought to their knees and their economic, their political, their social structure will come crashing down, for the house cleaning must be completed. Trust in your God, trust in My Words, My Prophets that have prophesied from ages past that all this will occur and God's Will will be done on Earth as it is in Heaven and Satan will be chained and will not deceive mankind again, for Love will rule, Love will conquer the hearts of man and Love will reign and with Love in all hearts the whole Earth will be renewed and all will be full of My Spirit and I will walk among you, so rejoice, My son, and tell all My Children of the Good News that soon all this will occur and to persevere, to trust, to be abandoned to God's Holy Providence for their lives, to pray for souls, to love all, to be lights in the darkness, to practice the teachings of the Divine Will so they will be ready to live in the new Era. Tell them not to hold onto the present, the world will all change. So live for the future and be at peace, for I am and I have everything in control and My Will will be done - FIAT. I love you, My Son of My Divine Will."

"I love You, my Lord and my God."

"...LOVE US WITH THE LOVE OF YOUR NEW WILL..."
May 5, 1994 AM 11:30

"My dear child, I love you. Give Me your will. I will take it and place it at the Throne of the Divine God. I will give God's Holy Will to you."

"I give you my will, Mommy."

"I want you, my child, in the Kingdom fully with no ties to this Earth, no ties to your will, so continue to implement the teachings and now I have your will in a more complete fashion. Keep giving it to me, it must be removed completely, even the roots. My child, love my Son Jesus, my Lord and Savior, love your Mother. You are my child, love God the Father, love the Holy Spirit, love Us with the love of your new Will, God's Will, the perfect Love of the Creator, for now your will is God's Will and you can love Us with His, not your old will. Peter, We have so few that love Us, so be special, be a perfect Son of the Divine Will. Up now, back to your work."

"I love you mommy."

"I love you, my Son of the Divine Will."

"IT WILL CONTROL AND DIRECT YOU IN THE WORLD TO ALWAYS DO GOD'S WILL IN ALL CIRCUMSTANCES..." May 5, 1994 PM 11:30

"My dear child, you are one with the Heart of my Son, you are one with the Heart of your Mother, you are one in the Divine Will. Blessed is the house of Israel, blessed is the House of the Lord, for all things come in big packages with God, big packages full of gifts, but the biggest gift is the gift of the Divine Will indwelling in your being, for It is there within you, It will control and direct you in the world to always do God's Will in all circumstances and all situations, so let It by being a nothing and having no will of your own. So rest now, my son, we will talk tomorrow. I love you Peter."

"I love you, Mommy."

"...YOU MUST BE AWARE OF YOUR THOUGHTS..." May 5, 1994 PM 05:30

"My son, I love you, I want you to know that all the love in the world is inside you and you're in charge of letting it out. That means you have to live in the Divine Will. It has to come out unrestricted without any blockage, so Peter, don't

hinder it with thoughts about yourself, about your life, about the happenings in your work life..."

"Help me Lord."

"...I will, but you must be aware of your thoughts and be constantly killing them, for they are not from Me, so they are from either your will or the evil one, so rid your mind of them. Also, My son, don't be concerned about whether you are or are not lazy. I am running the show, the schedule. You are not lazy, you are working for Me, I set up the circumstances, I will provide the funds you need to provide for your family. You don't have to work 12 hours a day. I will make sure you work the right number of hours to make the right amount of money to provide for your family. So Peter, just live moment by moment and be My Soldier of Love, time is too short and I need you to love, to carry and deliver My Love to My Children. Peace, My son, tonight will be special, I will be there with Mom and Dad and of course the Holy Spirit. I love you, My Son of My Will."

"I love You, my King."

"...TO GROW LOVE IN A SOUL, YOU MUST BE A GARDENER OF LOVE..." May 6, 1994 AM 06:00

"My dear child, please don't think you are not worthy of your calling, for you are My Slave and I am guiding and directing you and you are a nothing and God is everything. So your part is the "zero" and God the Father, Jesus your Brother and the Holy Spirit make up for your nothingness. So Peter, you only have to live the teachings and then you will be great but it won't be you, it will be the Divine shining through in all ways. Peter, it is so important to live the moment, to stay focused on the activities of the moment, to respond to inspirations of the moment, to listen in conversations and love the others you are with. So, My son, make this your focus of your day, to live the moment, to divide the day in segments, to love Us and love souls and forget everything else. My dear child, live in Our Hearts, they are rooms you can walk in

anytime of the day or night and receive Our Love, Our Care, Our Concern, Our Encouragement, Our Graces to continue your mission of love with peace, with determination, with perseverance. Stay in these rooms all day and We will support you. Peter, Love has three steps, three phases; they are to plant the seed, second, to water it, and third, to fertilize it. So, to make, to grow love in a soul, you must be a gardener of love and you must nurture the souls We place in your path and God is Love and the garden is the world and the plants are the souls. So, My son, don't get in the way, let Our Love flow through you to all the plants and We will use you as Our Gardener, so make sure you live the moment and then We can guide and direct you and speak through you and say all the right things and be what the souls need at their particular stage in growth. I love you, My dear child, walk with Us today, be Ours, love Us and forget yourself, fall back in Our Arms and We will take care of everything so you can be used as Our Gardener of Love."

"I love you, my Queen, my Mother."

"...THANK YOU FOR LETTING ME USE YOU" May 8, 1994 AM 00:45

"My dear child, thank you for your abandonment, thank you for your trust, thank you for letting me use you. The fruits were many and there will be many more, so Peter, continue on your mission of love. I will take care of everything so you can be led by me to do the Father's Will. I love you, my dear child."

"I love you, my Mother, my Mommy."

"...LIVE TODAY AND EVERY DAY IN THE MOMENT..." May 8, 1994 AM 06:00

"My son, be Mine, be full of My Spirit, be one with My Will. Have no cares of the world, be little, be loving, be a son that wants to please his Father, a little brother that wants to imitate his big brother. Peter, live the teachings, make them

your life so that you can please Us. Hold in front of you always that this world is dying and to be a part of it is non-productive. You were born for eternal life, so let not this world upset you in any way. My son, I love you and I am God and am in control of everything. Peter, live today and every day in the moment and love those you will be with. Live the moment and repeat the ejaculatory prayers. Live the moment and stay in a steady, calm, serene state, live the moment and follow all Our Inspirations. Be led by the Holy Spirit. My child, I love you and want you to stay little so that We can have a close intimate relationship and you can love Me and I can love and care for you in every way. So, stay focused, strive to have God's Will reign, strive to live in God's Will and then you will do God's Will and you will be infinitely joyful and content and We will be very pleased to have you as a Son of Our Divine Will. Go now, My son, and start the day. Live with Us, live for Us, live in Our Hearts and be a shining 'son' in a dark world. I love you Peter."

"I love You, my Lord and my God."

"...USE THESE KEYS TO OPEN UP THE LOCKED DOORS OF THE HEARTS OF OTHERS..." May 8, 1994 PM 05:00

"My dear child, Love will be on top, on top of all other desires of your will if you put it first, if you want it, if you make it number one in your life, if you are one with your God and love is where all your desires for other's needs are changed into desires with the right intentions, for love is the heart of your soul and love is what makes a creature Divine, love is what makes a creature stand out and shine among others for without love there is a reflection of self, a reflection of evil desires, a reflection of a rotten heart, a heart that smells of the world. So nurture love in your heart and you will be nurturing the Spirit of God, the Spirit of Love, the Spirit of Wisdom, the Spirit of Everlasting Omnipotent Desire that God has for love of you and for all creatures. My child, love is the

focus, love is the key. It is what unlocks the doors to hearts that are locked shut by the evil one by self-centeredness. It is as important as an Earthly key is to a storehouse of gold and precious gems. My child, you have a key chain with keys of love and you must use these keys to open up the locked doors of the hearts of others I place you with. My child, if you are wrapped up in your Earthly life, then you tie your hands and stop the key from ever being used, so, My son, trust Us for all your Earthly needs and cares and then you can be Our Locksmith. We will teach you the art of opening even the most securely locked doors of sinner's hearts. Peter, the keys you will use will be fabricated out of the purest love, the Love from my and my Son's Hearts. They will be keys stamped with Our Coat of Arms, Our Two Hearts, and without a doubt the keys will unlock the most secure doors. So, my child, be Our Locksmith, be Our Evangelist, be Our Special Child of the Father's Will that will be obedient to Our Inspiration and act and do when We call you to unlock the doors of God's hardened and rebelling Children. I love you, my dear child."

"I love you, my Mother, my Mommy."

"...YOU MUST BE REBORN IN THE DIVINE WILL..."
May 9, 1994 AM 05:45

"My son, Oh how I love all who strive to do the Will of the Father! Oh how I desire to live in their hearts and hold them close in My Arms! My son, do you want to please Me greatly? Then do My Holy Will, do It with love, joy and peace. My son, the main thrust of your efforts is to be inspired by My indwelling Divine Will, for this is the gift, this is the grace that will aid you in your efforts to do His Glorious, Omnipotent and Everlasting Will. My son, persevere, stay committed, you must change your habits, you must be reborn in the Divine Will and kill once and for all your own will, for it is only possible by having God's indwelling Will in control in place of your will that you will always do God's Holy Will in all the actions and deeds of your life. Peter, it is not going

to happen overnight, for this is going to take time, but if you are living with the right attitude then you will practice with your life's activities, with your life's trials, with your life's vocation. So, My son, become My Son of My Will by striving to be a nothing, a little child and to be filled with the new teachings of the Divine Will. Peter, I am by your side, so is Mom and We want you completely abandoned to the Will. Practice living in the moment and listening and acting on inspirations We give you to live in and do the Will of the Father. I love you, Peter, start the day but be full of joy and peace. Be on vacation from the world and you will see, you will have a lovely day living in the Kingdom."

"I love You, my King, my Savior, my Lord, my God."

"...I WILL INSPIRE YOU..." May 9, 1994 AM 08:45

"My son, I will inspire you, what to do today and when to do it. I will inspire you, what to say to those I place in your path and all the work that needs to be done today will get done. So now, My son, you can live in My Will, do My Will and love Me and love others. Peace, My son, We go together."

"I love You, my Lord, my King, my Comforter, my Best Friend."

"...THE TRIUMPH OF LOVE, THE UNION OF ALL HEARTS IN GOD'S LOVE!" Mar 9, 1994 AM 11:00

"My son, to love Me is to love your Mother, is to love the Father, is to love the Holy Spirit, for to love Me you are exercising the gift of love that I have given you and the gift of love is from God and God is Love and when you love Us you return this love to Us that We have given you. This is union with your Divine Family. Love is union with God and love of God is love of the infinite, love of the Almighty, love of He who is, so, My son, love Me by loving all of Us together in the unity of God's Love. Peter, love is the Treasure House of God's Kingdom. In the treasure house resides there the fruits *of the Spirit for God's Spirit is Love and it is without a beginning or an end and it encloses all, it is for all and with all that dwell in the Kingdom of God, all that have, live in, and do His Will. Peter, be united with all in love. It is the perfect media to connect to, bond to, share in the lives of others, to console, to care, to help, to listen, to nurture and direct their souls back to the focus of Our existence, which is to love the Trinity, to love the Family, the Body of Christ with the Love of God. Peace, My son, joy, My son, rejoice, My son, for Love is It, It is without limits, without end, It is the Heart of the Soul of God and He wants all to have and share It and hence the Triumph of Love, the union of all hearts in God's Love! Hallelujah! The Father's Plan defined, the Father's Will explained and His Will will be done - FIAT. My Love for you is incomprehensible, it is united to, it is a part of, it is one with God the Father's Love. Carry on, My son, back to your mission of love."*

"I love You, my King, my Lord of Love."

"...BECOME A STRAIGHT 'A' STUDENT OF THE DIVINE WILL AND YOU WILL GRADUATE WITH A PhD IN THE LOVE OF GOD" May 9, 1994 PM 11:45

"My son, I love you, peace be with you. My son, the Love of God is the root of the tree of life, it is the passage where life flows, it is the strength that holds the tree in place, it is the part of the tree that is essential to the tree's life for with no roots the tree is not nourished, the tree will be blown down with the least of winds. My son, your soul needs to have roots to My Heart so that your soul becomes a tree of life that grows to fullness, that grows to towering heights, a tree that provides shade to those in need of rest, a tree that is strong and stable, that is immovable, a tree with roots that will connect and be a conduit of pure love to nourish and provide all the tree's needs. My son, your being must be all Mine, it must be fully possessed by My Spirit of Love, it must be totally transformed into a burning Sun that warms all that come near

it with the Love of God. Peter, think of yourself as only an atom of your being that is a part of your being which is totally possessed by My Spirit, My Will, My Heart, My Mother's Heart and your being will be a power plant of Divine Energy that electrocutes others with the power of Divine Love and this love will be so great that it will short circuit to others and will fill others with this Divine Energy, this Divine Power, this Divine Love, the Love of God. Peter, what is necessary for this transformation of your being to take place? It will occur when you perfect the teachings of the Divine Will, for your being will be directed by God's indwelling Will, your being will be living in God's Holy Will, your being will be doing God's Will and as such, you will be in complete union with the Will of God, you will be a docile, an obedient, a perfect image of Jesus. You will be a walking flame of God's Holy Spirit, you will be a nothing and God will be everything. So, My son, strive to learn, practice and become a straight 'A' student of the Divine Will and you will graduate with a P.H.D. in the Love of God and I will hire you for the rest of your life on this Earth and you will be paid with the Divine Payments of My Love and Care to the amount necessary to keep you on fire, fully inflamed with constant heat of the Love of God. You will receive the Peace of God, the Joy of God and the assurance of a retirement for all eternity with Me and the Family in Heaven. Oh what a prize, Oh what a gift, Oh what a perfect plan for your future! Have it, live it, do it, My Son of the Father's perfect, glorious, omnipotent and all knowing Divine Will - sleep in My Arms with your head on My Heart, I love you Peter."

"I love You, my All, my God, my King, my Savior, my Teacher, thank you."

"...YOU MUST BE ONE HUNDRED AND TEN PERCENT COMMITTED" May 10, 1994 AM 06:00

"My son, happy are those who live in and do the Will of the Father, for their efforts, their persistence goes not

unnoticed. My son, it is in this effort they make that draws them into the Divine Light of the Will of God, a light so bright as to outshine the Sun. This light surrounds the Creator, this light envelops the creature, this light keeps the evil one at bay. My son, something of great value is obtained gradually, something built strong and stable must have a good foundation, something learned slowly is absorbed and not forgotten. So, My son, to become an adult Son or Daughter of the Divine Will will take time but the investment is of high return. My son, you must be one hundred and ten percent committed, you must have the grace of perseverance, you must be focused and detached from creature's wants and desires, from material wants and possessions. You must not be distracted from your efforts by the world and its pulls or by the devil and evil pleasures. My son, happy are those who run the race, who exercise self discipline in their training, for they will cross the finish line, they will win the gold medal, they will receive a crown with stars of light, they will be one with the Father, one with the Son, one with the Holy Spirit, for their will will be Divine, they will have God's Holy Will, they will live in God's Holy Will, they will do God's Holy Will each day of their life and for all eternity. My son, keep up the pace, don't slow down and you will glow in the light and the love of the Divine. Start your day now. My son, be united to the Trinity, be one with your God, be full of the Holy Spirit of Love, carry your cross with the Savior. I love you Peter, We go together."

"I love You, my Lord, my God."

"THIS IS WHY I STRETCH YOU OUT FINANCIALLY...I AM TEACHING YOU TO LIVE IN MY WILL" May 10, 1994 PM 01:00

"My son, to worry is to be out of the Will of God, for worry comes from the human will. Worry is anxiety, worry is association with doubting and all are products of the human will. They are products of human pride, for to think that you can control the future, can control circumstances, can control

others is a step out in pride, not a step out in faith, not a lesson in trust but a lesson in depending on self and this is intolerable to God. He won't have it, His children must have faith, must trust, must totally depend on Him for everything, their food, clothing, shelter, protection, everything, for He is the Father and the human creatures are His children. The other creatures of God, the birds, the animals, the fish, all have no wills of their own and as a result they are at peace, they depend on God for everything, they live and do His Will because they are inspired by the Divine Will. My son, do you worry about your heart beating, do you worry about getting in an auto accident, do you worry about falling down the stairs, do you worry about breaking your back?"

"No, I don't."

"Well, why do you worry about paying bills? - because you have pride, you think you are in control of your future, you think you can control your destiny. Well, all of the other items I mention could happen to you if it was My Will, but you don't worry, you trust Me that they will not happen to you. So, My son, it is humility you need, it is the realization that you can't control anything because you are not in control of how much money you make or where it will be spent, I am, for I love you and I am working on you, I am gently teaching you a lesson in humility. I am ridding your being of pride, I am molding you into a son that trusts in His Father to provide all his needs, even financial. So, My son, you must trust Me if you want this cross removed, you must become humble if you want this cross removed, you must know that I am omnipotent and almighty and am in control of every part, every detail of your life, including your financial needs. My son, I love you and the love I have is infinitely greater than the love that an Earthly Father has for his child and you are a little infant, a small baby and I am raising you and I am caring for you, so you must trust your Dad with your all for all your needs. This will please Me greatly, for then I will know you have no pride. You are My Little One that I can place on My Lap and

entertain and love and hug and kiss and your love for Me will be pure and you will love Me as a child, a little child loves his daddy. This is why I stretch you out financially, not because I can't provide, but because I am teaching you to live in My Will. I am teaching you the way to My Heart. I love you, My son, become My Humble Little Child and then My Heart will be full of joy. I love you Peter."

"Thank You, my Lord, my God, my All."

"...ALWAYS BE TRUTHFUL, ALWAYS DESIRE TO KNOW THE TRUTH..." May 10, 1994 AM 11:30

"My son Peter, I love you. How do you tell a lion from a tiger? - the stripes?, the hair about the face? Well, Peter, it is like this with the persons of the world, they are full of pride, full of anxiety, full of every evil vice. My son, the lion's hair hides the smallness of the head, it puts a damper on the truth from being received, for those of the world are always trying to deceive others. They think they are smarter than others and have no conscience of the truth. The way is only necessary to reach the ends in mind. Peter, deception is straight from Hell and to be a part of any deception is to be joined to Hell and when you touch fire you get burned. So, My son, you must stay in the truth in all your actions, in all your words and never deceive anyone. My son, John the Baptist died, was killed, because he spoke the truth and so with many martyrs. I described Myself as the Way, the Truth and the Life because of the value of the truth. When you talk to others you must always speak clearly, speak the truth, for not to is deceptive or a lie and the latter only pleases the evil one. There is only one truth and with the truth there is no confusion. With truth all can agree, with truth all can be of one mind, one heart, one spirit. With truth there is justice, with truth there is purity, with truth all must conform, for when the truth is determined or found, then all must agree. My son, to know the truth and not to follow it, not to implement it, not to adjust to it is to follow the evil one, is to live a lie and if

you do not love the truth then you will be in contradiction to God and He will punish by allowing you to be deceived by the evil one and you will fall into error. So, My son, always be truthful, always desire to know the truth, always strive to determine and search for the truth and you will be doing God's Will, your intentions will be right and you will not be led astray by the evil one but will stay in the light of the truth, the purity of the truth. I love you, My Son of My Will, have It, live It, do It, We go now together."

"I love You, my King."

"...YOU SHOULD ALWAYS BE AT PEACE AND IN A VERY JOYFUL STATE.." May 10, 1994 PM 07:45

"My dear child, I love you, this is your Mother, Jesus is my Lord and Savior, I bow down, I worship Him, He is my all! Peace be with you. Peter, tomorrow is another day to love Us and love souls. Each day that passes We get closer to the Father's Wrath, We get closer to the new Era, We get closer to the Kingdom coming on Earth as it is in Heaven. My child, you must pray for souls, you must offer up the unceasing 'Act', you must offer up your life to Me so that I can present it to the Father united to my Son's Life, my son's sacrifice, my Son's desires to please the God of Abraham. Peter, you are my special child. You must love others unconditionally, you must love others with my Heart, with my Son's Heart. You must love them divinely. This is your calling, one of love. Share His Love, spread His Love, for Love will triumph, it will win. This is God's Will for the Earth. God the Father created all and He can make any changes He desires to and He loves His Creatures and is going to make the changes necessary in order that His Will will reign in all hearts, in all lives, in all of creation, for when men's hearts are changed then all will be in harmony. Peter, this is your future, this is your hope, this is what you are helping to bring to completion by the distribution of the Words you have been given and by implementing and making them your life you will contribute

greatly. My dear child, have entire peace about your mission, the schedule is planned out for each day until the Lord comes and thereafter. Your only concern is to live the teachings, mainly to love God, love others and do, live in and be inspired by God's Will in all your life's activities and your thoughts, words and actions. My dear child, you need not ever be anxious, you need not be troubled, perturbed or in any way upset. You should always be at peace and in a very joyful state even if you are carrying a heavy cross or being persecuted, for We will always be at your side and We will always be in control to the smallest detail of your life. This means, my son, that you can fall back in a state of constant abandonment, knowing that you are living in and doing God's Will. Peter, because these words have been given to you and you have this mission, you will always have others watching you and you will be an example to others in this regard, you will be a living example of the words, the teachings. This is a big responsibility and you therefore must not ever slip backwards but always progress in making the teachings your life in every way. With this great responsibility comes also great graces, if you do your part and be docile and a little child, a little nothing with no pride, no selfishness. You must know that all that has been given to you is for God's Glory, not yours. Peter, live your calling in a state of wonderment, knowing that God's Love for you is infinite and that you are already in Heaven in the Kingdom of the Divine Will and that your main goal is to spread the Words of Love, Words of Peace, Words of Comfort, Words of Wisdom, Words of the Future, the new Era, the new Earth, the new Heaven established here on Earth. Peter, I love you, stay in my Heart, cling to me, depend on me, be my little child, let me hold your hand and guide you and teach you in the Love, in the Will, in the Joy of the Trinity."

"I love you, my Mommy, I am yours."

"...HAVE A BEAUTIFUL DAY TODAY LIVING IN OUR WILL" May 11, 1994 AM 05:45

"My son, I love you, have a beautiful day today living in Our Will. Live abandoned to all that happens, knowing that We are in control, live moment by moment, live it intensely, inflamed in love for your Divine Family and for all creatures you are placed with or that are placed in your path. Live in a state of peace, calm, serenity, have no worries or doubts, have only trust in the love of God and total dependence in Divine Providence for your life's needs. Peter, strive to pray without ceasing, repeat the ejaculatory prayers, talk to Us all day long, talk to Us from your heart, ask Us what to do and when to do it. Let the Will of God reign and have no will of your own. Let It reign in all your thoughts, actions, acts. My son, all We desire from you is love, please stay focused on this. Everything and everybody are as nothing in comparison to the love you should always have for your Divine Family. So, My son, remain lost in peace, love and joy throughout the day and We will walk, talk, and listen to you wherever you go and whatever you do. The Father loves you, I love you, the Holy Spirit loves you, Mary your Mother loves you, all the Angels and Saints love you, all together united to the Will and the Love of God."

"I love You, my Divine Family, united also to the Will and Love of God and I give you my will and my fiat, my all."

"PETER, YOU ARE A MESSENGER OF HOPE..." May 13, 1994 AM 06:00

"My son, My Apostle, you must connect as you did tonight with others and share the Word, for the Word is God. My son, this will draw you and the others closer to the Divine. Peter, trust that I will give you the insight and wisdom to share and to be in the truth. Peter, I am God, I am the Creator, I am in control of the future, I reveal My Plans of the future to prophets. You are a prophet, you have been chosen to comfort My children in these troubled times, you have been chosen to

inform My people of the great hope in the future, My Kingdom is coming, My Will will be done on Earth as it is in Heaven. I will deliver My children from evil, Satan will be chained and he and all his followers will be sent back to Hell, never to torment and destroy My Creation again. Peter, you are a messenger of hope and through you My Words will inform My Children that I am in control and to trust in God's Providence for their lives and God's Providence is to bring all His children into His Embrace, into His Divine Will, into His Everlasting Love He has for each and every one. For the Love of the Trinity is Divine Love and Love will triumph in the hearts of all mankind. Peace, My son, joy, My son, your enslavement in this material world is almost over. Soon all will trust in their God for all their needs as do all My other creatures and there will be harmony, there will be love, there will be the realization, the accomplishment of the Holy, Just, Right Will of God. Peter, live moment by moment in a state of tranquility, peace, knowing that I support you as the air you breathe, I love you as the Son of My Offspring, a Son of My Divine Will. Peter, have absolutely no fear of the future, for you are in My Hands and protected in My and My Mother's Heart so start the day, live the day, end the day in joy and fulfill your mission of love as I inspire you moment by moment. I love you, My son of My Will. Go now, start your adventure to find Me in others and love Me there where I dwell also and you will be living love, living union, the union of hearts in the Love of God."

"I love You, my King of Love, thank you for your words."

"You're welcome, My son, keep up the pressure to change and become a pure, refined diamond of My Love that will reflect My Love to all you come in contact with."

"THESE WORDS ARE SPIRIT AND LIFE, SPIRIT OF LOVE AND LIFE OF NEW CREATION IN THE HEARTS OF MY CHILDREN" *May 13, 1994 PM 00:30*

"My son, how happy I am that the book will be out soon![6] *The light will shine, the doors will open, the Sun will rise, the torch will be lit, the candle will burn, the fire will enkindle! My son, thank you for your efforts. My Words now can touch hearts and spark the Love of God that resides there into a fiery furnace. You will see the results. These Words are Spirit and Life, Spirit of Love and Life of New Creation in the hearts of My children. Peter, without doubt, without worry, without hesitancy proceed to follow the inspiration that you receive to plant these books into the hands of key children of My Mother's Army and they will join with you to spread the word that Love will Triumph in the hearts of mankind and evil will lose and be vanquished from the surface of the Earth. So start the snowball rolling and watch it grow and gain the momentum and nothing will stop the force of My Love, for Love is God and God is Love and God is omnipotent and all must join in or be swept away by the storm and with these words direction will be given, guidance will be given, motivation will be given, inspiration will be given, hearts will be warmed and union will be obtained between My Children and between My Heart and My Children's hearts so rejoice, My son, be joyful, have My Spirit, My Spirit of Triumphant Love and spread It and share It with all you meet. I love you, My Soldier, My Apostle, My Son of My Will."*

"Thank You, my King, I love You."

"YOU MUST BE A LITTLE CHILD...DON'T BE CHILDISH BUT HAVE THE FAITH, TRUST AND LOVE THAT A CHILD HAS..." May 13, 1994 PM 11:30

"My son, happy are those who strive to be one with the Trinity, for there in the union is the Divine, the Everlasting Love of God and this union is the union of the heart of the creature with the Heart of God. My son, to be united to the

---

[6] "The Triumph of Love"

Trinity is to be one with the Will of God and the Will of God is that of Love for Love wills that all be united in this bond, this eternal bond, this bond of love between hearts. My son, happy are those who strive to do the Will of the Trinity, for their intentions will be recognized and grace will be poured out upon them. They will be filled with God's Love and this Love will unite them to the Trinity, the Father, Son and Holy Spirit. My son, to be a Son or Daughter of God's Holy Will is to be one in every way with the Triune God. You must have no will of your own, you must live the teachings, you must be a little child with no pride. Peter, live as a child with your Divine Family, don't be childish but have the faith, trust and love that a child has in and with his Father and Mother, a faith that knows no different or other way than what he is told, a gullible faith, a blind faith, an unquestioning faith. Have the trust of a child, a trust that knows Daddy or Mommy will care for him or her, a trust that knows he or she will be protected from all evil, a trust that knows that Father knows best and will always have the answer, the correct answer, a trust that is unwavering, for the child is little, is uneducated and knows he or she is not capable of running his or her life and therefore trusts in Daddy for all direction and guidance for his or her life. Have the love of a child, an innocent love with no self-love, no deceit, no self interest, a love that is pure, a love that comes straight from the heart, the heart of a child. A child wants to always be held in the arms of the Daddy or Mommy to hug them, to be close and depend on them. A child always wants their love when he or she gets hurt or is sorry for something he or she has done wrong and the Daddy or Mommy can't resist and fills them with love because of the child's innocence, because love is the cure for all the problems and growth pains of the child. For the child is raised on love and needs love and this is the bond between the Daddy and the Mommy and the child. So be a child, My son, and enjoy and nurture the bond of love between your Daddy, your Mother, your Brother and the Holy Spirit. Have no pride, be a little one and the bond of love will flourish, will grow, will become a union of love between hearts that no one or no thing or no desire or want will be able to separate and you will be a true Child of God, a Child of the Father's Will, a Child of the Father's Heart, a Child that is the apple of the Father's Eye. Oh My son, be united to your Divine Family with this bond, this everlasting bond of Love. I love you, My son, begin the day, hold Our hands as a child and We will guide you and be with you in all your activities, all your conversations, all your thoughts. It will be a day of love, a day with your Family, We will rest in your heart and you will rest in Ours."

"I love You, my Divine Family."

"...MY CHILDREN MUST HAVE HOPE IN THE FUTURE" May 14, 1994 PM 02:00

"My dear child, this is your Mother, I love you, Jesus is my Lord and Savior! Thank you for your work on the next book. You must get this second book out as quickly as possible also, for my children must have hope in the future. They must have these words to reinforce them, strengthen them and get them through the storm, for with these words they will see the vision of the future, they will know that the end of the rainbow is waiting and that they must persevere and abandon themselves to God's Holy Providence. My child, the trial itself will be a teaching in the Divine Will, for all of my children will have to trust totally in God the Father. They will have to be detached from everything, they will have to be led and inspired to live in and do God's Holy Will. All they will need is their rock, their God, for all other support will be removed. Unless my children are prepared for this, unless they have the right attitude, then they may be swept away by the storm from following their own will. They must let God's Holy Will reign, not their own, they must stay in my Heart, they must stay in prayer, they must not get caught in the confusion of the trial. They will not be in control, no human being will be, this will be quite explicit. God the Father will be in control, His Will

will rule and if you let His Will reign and implement the teachings, then you will realize each day, each hour that with His Will peace of heart will be yours and with peace you will be able to love others that are troubled and bring them back to my Son. Peter, I love you, I am your spiritual Mommy, I want to help you grow, I want to teach you the way to Daddy's Heart, so let me by asking me to help you and guide you. This will draw you closer to me and to our Divine Family. Peter, time will pass quickly, before you know it the new Era will be here. God's Will will be done. No one, no government, no organization will be able to stop God from implementing His Plan, so Peter, go with the flow, swim with the current, drift with the tide, live moment by moment and have my peace which is the Peace of my Son, the Peace of the Father, the Peace of the Holy Spirit, the Peace of living in His Will. Thank you in advance for all your work, I love you, my child, and I embrace you and will be caring for you and your family always for you are in my Heart and my Heart is a refuge and my Heart will protect you and guide you all the days of your life."

"I love you Mommy, thank you."

"You're welcome. Carry on with your daily duties, clean that desk, make your wife happy!"

"THE NEW ERA WILL BE A NEW EARTH, A NEW HEAVEN..." May 14, 1994 PM 11:00

"My son, Oh how happy you would be to see, touch and love all those who live in Heaven, for your homeland awaits you! What a glorious place, a place of stars, a place of great light, a place to share, to love, to worship and praise the Trinity! My son, soon you will be in Heaven. This life will end soon and the new Era will begin, for life as you know it will die. The new Era will be a new Earth, a new Heaven, where all is done in accordance to the Will of the Father. My son, happy are those who persevere, who hold out, who deny their wills and invite My Will, the Will of the Father, to live in their being. My son, the Father's is one of perfection, is one

of great love. His Will is to save His Flock, His children and bring them home to a renewed Earth where all will live with grace, love, joy and peace, where all will be totally committed to loving the Trinity and loving others with the Love of the Trinity. My son, it's just around the corner, just over the hill, just through the storm, just through the gate and then Bingo!, the jack pot at the end of the rainbow, the land of the Father's Love lived and practiced between all hearts, the complete and detailed Design of God for the creature will be realized. Hold onto this vision, see through the darkness, through the haze, through the mystery of the world. Have the eternal gaze of the future, the dream come true, for slavery will end and freedom will begin, all families will produce flowers of love, flowers of purity, flowers for the Father, Son and Holy Spirit. All will rest in the Love, Care and Peace of the Trinity. It will be marvelous, it will be Divine, it will be the best of the best, for all will be inflamed in the Love and the Will of God! Peter, hope in the future, live for the future, live one day at a time, one moment to the next and soon you will see the total and complete transformation of the hearts of mankind. I love you, My son of My Will, My Messenger of Good News, My Apostle of the new Era. Rest now in My Heart, in My Love, in My Will."

"I love You, my King."

"HAVE A BEAUTIFUL DAY IN THE KINGDOM..." May 15, 1994 AM 06:00

"My son, have a beautiful day in the Kingdom, for to do God's Will, live in His Will and be inspired by and let His Will reign is Heaven on Earth! My son, have a beautiful day in the Heart of your Savior lost in endless love, the Love of the Sacred Heart enclosing you, caring for you, joining you to love! My son, have a beautiful day in the Immaculate Heart of the Queen keeping you in a garden of purity of heart, mind and soul, giving you strength to resist temptation and rid sin from your life, putting enmity between you and the evil one by being

joined to your Mother's Heart! My son, have a beautiful day filled with the Holy Spirit of Triumphant Love, drowned in an ocean of love, overwhelmed by flames of love melted into pure and precious gold of love filled with explosive Divine Love! My son, have a beautiful day letting God's Holy, Glorious, Omnipotent Eternal Will reign in all your thoughts, words, actions, acts each moment, each hour of the day! My son, have a beautiful day in communion with all your older brothers and sisters in Heaven and in Purgatory, united to their love and worship of the Trinity! My son, have a beautiful day walking with your angels guarding and protecting you, guiding and directing you, filling you with inspirations to do the Holy Will of the Father! My son, live in the Divine, live in the Kingdom, live in God's Will, live in peace, live in harmony with all of creation, live in joyful hope of the future! My son, trust Me for everything you need, trust Me to care for you, trust Me to be your best friend! Pray without ceasing, pray for souls, for priests, pray for all you come in contact with and share My Love, shine with My Love, burn and crack hearts with My Love! Another day, My son, in the Kingdom, begin, proceed, start and live your mission of triumphant love. We will be with you so go now, I love you Peter."

"I love You, my Lord and my God."

"REALIZE THE POWER YOU HAVE NOW AT YOUR CALLING" May 15, 1994 PM 02:00

"My son, to live united to My Will is to have no will of your own, this is basic, but to live united to My Heart is to unite your heart to Mine and to live united to My Mother's Heart is to unite your heart to her's. My son, to love with Our Hearts is to unite to the Love of God from Our Hearts. This love is pure, this love is divine, this love is powerful. My son, you have this love at your disposal, for you are united to Our Hearts, therefore, when you come in contact with others, when you are with others, depend on this love, release this love, become this love and you will realize that the love that is

within you is great, is endless, is free flowing. So, My son, realize this in a big way and be a Soldier of Love to all you meet. My son, My Will now dwells inside you because you have made the consecration. Therefore, use It, not your own. Realize this and you will be able to have the confidence that your life is being run by the Father's Will if you always follow our inspirations given moment by moment. This is a very powerful resource, have great confidence in it. Trust in God's indwelling Will for direction and the scheduling of every day's activities and as you do, you will cease to have a will of your own. The sooner you rid your being of your own will in a complete way, the sooner you can become totally confident that God's Holy Will is in complete control. Continue to implement the teachings to accomplish this. My son, I love you very much and I want you to realize the power you have now at your calling. The access to this power is obtained by living the teachings, mainly by being an absolute nothing and by living moment by moment and praying unceasingly. So, My son, follow through, perfect the lessons you have been given and you will give glory to the Trinity in a great way. Peace, My son, Love, My son, Joy, My son, it is yours! Go now, My Son of My Divine Will, My Son of My Heart, My Son of My Mother's Heart, back to your mission of triumphant love in the Kingdom of the Divine Will."

"I love You, my Lord, thank You."

"You're welcome, leave Me with your will and go."

"WALK CLOSER AND CLOSER TO ME EACH DAY" May 15, 1994 PM 11:30

"My dear child, I love you, this is your Mother, I bow down to Jesus, my Lord, the King of Kings, Lord of Lords! Please pray for souls, time is so short now. Soon my time for pleading with my children will be over and the Father's Wrath will commence. Peter, it will be a great demonstration that God is in control of all, it will be a devastating blow to your country, they will not recover. My dear child, you must pray

110

for souls and tell others also. All will change drastically but know all is in God's Hands. You will be safe in my Heart and so will your family for you and they are one in the Father's Eyes. Peter, I love you and want you to walk closer and closer to me each day. Do this by your dependence on my motherly care and protection. Ask me to pray for your intentions and for others that ask you to pray for them. I am a real prayer warrior and can pray with you and for you in this way. My child, give me your family. I will place them in my Heart and there they will be sheltered and protected. My child, ask me to guide you in your spiritual growth and for lessons in the Divine Will. My child, I am with you to raise you to be pleasing in the Father's Eyes. Peter, with time will come the conversion of all peoples to the one true church. This will be a great event but now the church is in turmoil and much confusion, for the evil one is leading many astray. Have no fear, scripture must be fulfilled, the great apostasy must occur. Peter, live without worry, care or desires for material wants and possessions. Live in peace, in joy, in love. It will be a constant drag on you to strive to live the teachings but you must persevere. Thank you for your efforts to date. Keep it up and you will change your habits. They will go with your human will. Go now and start your day, live closer to Us every moment. I love you my child."

"I love you, my Mommy."

"...IF IT WERE NOT FOR THIS MISSION YOU WOULD HAVE BEEN IN HEAVEN A LONG TIME AGO" May 16, 1994 AM 11:00

"My son, give all glory, praise and honor to God the Father, the Almighty. Give your life to His Service, your heart to His Love, your spirit to His Spirit, unite your all with His, become a nothing, have nothing, let nothing hold you down, have no thought about your well-being; physically, spiritually or financially, it is all Ours. Care only to please the Trinity. Peter, My Son of My Will, you have Our Will, Our Heart, Our

Spirit, Our Love. It is yours, We are yours, We love you and embrace you and take full responsibility for you physically, spiritually and financially in every way, in every detail. Don't waste an instant caring about yourself, you need not, We will. We need you, We want you to be focused on your desire to only do Our Will, only love Us, only be united to Us. Now, My son, be joyful, at peace, full of Divine Life and Divine Love. Explode with the wonder of it all, live in the clouds above the world, live in the ocean of Our Love for you, live in the peace that is yours that only We can give, live each moment, live the adventure, the adventure of love, the mission of love that you have been assigned to undertake, for if it were not for this mission you would have been in Heaven a long time ago. We would rather have you up here than down there but you are called, you have given your Fiat, so pick up your crosses, pick them up joyfully, pick them up with love and go out into the world for Us, with Us and save souls. We love you, We need you, We await your return to the homeland. Return to your mission of love."

"I love You, my King, thank You."

"Carry on Peter."

"...IT IS UP TO YOU TO BE COMMITTED. YOU MUST BE FOCUSED ON GOD'S WILL" May 16, 1994 PM 10:00

"My son, I love you. Please be careful not to slip and do your own will. It happens when you are not at peace. It happens when you are full of pride. It happens when you are angry. It happens when you are not living in the Will of God. So, My son, always be on guard, continue mortifying your own will and the traits of your own will. Be at peace, be humble, be meek, be calm and God's Will will reign in you. Peter, have a hungry heart for the Love of God, always seek union of your will, your heart, your spirit to God's Will, Heart and Spirit and then God's Love will reign in your life. Peter, it is up to you to be committed. You must be focused on God's Will, so be challenged, be motivated, be sure that to have, live

and do the Will of God is the best of the best, the ultimate goal, the grand prize, the end of the rainbow and if you maintain this perspective you will always have your priorities straight, you will always be on your way to living as God desires His creatures to live and you will be pleasing the Father, Son and Holy Spirit in every way. There will be no conflict with your will and the Father's Will for only one Will will exist. Peter, yesterday is over, start anew. Make this day the best one yet by staying focused. I will help you. I know you are weak but you have Our Will, Our Hearts, Our Spirit. All you have to do is get rid of your own will. I love you Peter, be a nothing, live the moment, pray unceasingly and love, love, love."

"I love You, my King, my Savior, thank You."
"Peace, My son."

"...PLACE THE BOOK IN THE HANDS OF ALL MY CHILDREN..." May 17, 1994 PM 05:00

"My son, I love you. I am excited![7] I needed you to write this book. Now I need you to distribute this book. I chose you for this because you love Me and would do what I asked. Thank you Peter, this is what I would like to be done. Now place the book in the hands of all My children, the children of My and My Mother's Heart. They will receive it with joy and become inflamed with My Love for these are words of love. Peter, I love all My children and want them to live by faith, but these are special times and I am acting in this and other unusual ways to gather My Flock into My Heart, for there they will find rest, peace, love that will outweigh all the turmoil of the world. It is this turmoil that is necessary to bring the drastic changes to the hearts of My Children, for if I did not intervene the world would self-destruct and My Children would be left without any hope. Now they have hope.

---

[7] At a highway rest stop on the way back from picking up the first printing run of "The Triumph of Love".

113

Now they will know My Plan. Now they will trust in My Love. Now they will have the vision of the calm after the storm. These words have been saved until now because My Children would not have grasped them if the conditions were not right. Now the conditions are right and the events will happen so fast that My Children will all wake up. They will wake up to find these words to tell them that I am in control, that I love them, that I care for them, that I will bring them into My Heart and then to Paradise either on this Earth in the new Era or straight to their homeland. Peter, that bird is My creation, you are My creation, you are a lot more important than it. I care for the bird each moment of its life and I also care for you each moment of your life so trust Me and love Me and care not about yourself, only about loving Me and loving others. Go now, back to your Earthly home, We go together, I love you Peter."

"I love You, my Lord."

"MY SPIRIT IS THE LIFE OF YOUR BEING. IT IS WHY YOU GET SO EXCITED ABOUT SERVING ME" May 17, 1994 PM 11:00

"My son, I love you. Happy are those who live in and do My Will, for their reward will be great for all eternity. My son, have all the peace in the world, all the love in the world, all the joy in the world. Peter, all are yours, all of the peace, love, joy reside in you for My Spirit resides in you permanently. Peter, My Spirit is the life of your being. It is why you get so excited about serving Me, about loving Me. My Spirit is very powerful, It lives in you and you are Its carrier, you are Its temple, you are Its vessel. My Spirit loves others through you, for God's Love was created to be given and shared between the hearts of all creatures. A being without the Holy Spirit is void of love, void of life. All that resides is self, is a love used only to obtain what it wants, all are objects of use, all others are used for what self needs or desires or wants. It is a carnal love, not a heavenly love, not

114

a love of God but a love of the human will. So know that My Spirit indwells inside you in full force and this love is pure and it has been given to you for the Glory of God, not the glory of self. Peter, My Spirit is Life and life is freshness, life is vitality, life is joyful. A creature with My Spirit has these qualities, for not to have My Spirit is to be earthly, full of vices and evil desires, full of death, full of negativity. The Spirit of God is given freely, it is given to transform the soul into a creature that loves, serves and worships the Trinity and loves others unconditionally, unselfishly and without the Spirit of God the creature could not do this. The human creature is not capable of these Divine Qualities. My son, God desires to recreate man into His Own Image, He gives His Heart, His Spirit and now His Will to the creature if the creature desires the same and if the creature is willing with his own free will to desire this transformation and denies self so the Divine can reign. The conversion process does not end with a one-time commitment and baptism. It is on-going for all of the creature's life, it is daily, it is hourly, it is minute by minute for the creature must deny his will, deny his or her wants and desires so that the Divine increases daily, hourly, minute by minute. A creature can not be partially committed without being full of interior stress, for the human will is at odds with God's Will, with God's Spirit and with God's Heart. So Peter, be one hundred and ten percent committed, be without a will of your own, want nothing, desire nothing and let only God's Love, God's Divine Love reign and you will have God's Spirit, God's Will, God's Peace, God's Joy and your life will be a witness to the supernatural and you will be used by God to love and do His Will, all for the greater Glory, Honor and Praise of the Trinity. I love you Peter, start your day, start your mission, start it and complete it empty of self and full of the Divine. "

"I love You, my Lord and Savior."

"...HAVE HOPE, FOR WITHOUT HOPE ALL SEEMS LOST, DEPRESSION WILL SET IN AND THE EVIL ONE WILL COME AND TAKE YOU AWAY WITH A BOMBARDMENT OF HOPELESS AND DEPRESSING THOUGHTS" May 18, 1994 PM 09:00

"My dear child, this is your Mother, Jesus is my Lord, my Savior, my All, Alleluia! All glory, honor, praise be to God the Father, God the Son, God the Holy Spirit. Peter, you are a child of God, you are a son of the Father's Will, you have His Will indwelling in you, you have His Spirit, His Heart, this part of you is Divine, it is all-powerful, it is extra special, extra powerful, extra for these times! My dear child, no one is going to be preparing for the trial, for it will be so shocking that all will be in a state of disarray including your family. I am telling you this ahead of time because I want you to be prepared, so you can be a rock of hope, of peace, of calmness. It will be important for my children to have hope, for without hope all seems lost, depression will set in and the evil one will come and take you away with a bombardment of hopeless and depressing thoughts. So, my son, you must be a rock, a column of hope, for you know that God is in control of everything, you know why God has allowed the tribulations, the disasters, you know that you and all of my children of my Heart will be protected from the evil one and that you will be protected from the Father's Wrath, you know that when the storm subsides that calm will ensue and the world will be reborn and renewed spiritually and physically. This new birth will be the answer to the prayer of my Son, the Kingdom of God will come and His Will will be done. There will be no evil, no sin and love will reign between all hearts. So, my son, be full of hope now and during the trial. See through the storm to the clear sky and the calm sea, the sea of love and peace. My Son will come and walk among you again, all of this awaits you, so rejoice!, be joyful!, be content no matter what happens, no matter what you lose during the storm, for God owns all and will care for all your needs. My children

116

will be stripped of all their things, all their idols, all their support, their false security, there will be no hope, no future except in God's Care and the plan of salvation through Our Lord Jesus Christ, Son of God. Peter, don't get gloomy, don't get depressed, don't get worried, don't get doubtful. You must have hope, trust, faith and total abandonment and depend on the providence of the Father and this includes the care and protection that I will have for you for this is His Will and His Will will be done - FIAT. My dear son, you have not begun to realize how much love the Divine Family has for you and all my children of my Heart. If you could realize this you would recognize that each moment each day is in the Father's Hands and His Love for you is far greater than the love an Earthly Father has for his children and He is in control of all of creation and He owns all and you are His child. All He desires is the love of a faithful son or daughter from each of His children, all He desires is that we do His Will in the present world. This is very hard for the creature with all the pulls of the world so God the Creator is going to re-adjust everything so He can have His children back all to Himself, so He can love them, care for them and be honored and worshipped by them. This is the plan, this is the future, this is the hope so stay on track, be at peace, the future is bright. God loves you as do all your Divine Family so relax, be calm and strive to learn the teachings and become a perfect Son of the Father's Will. I love you, my dear child, carry on with your day, your mission of love."

"I love you, my Queen, my Mother, my Mom."

"TRUST IN MY LOVE...FOR EVERYTHING MATERIALLY, SPIRITUALLY AND PHYSICALLY" May 19, 1994 AM 11:00

"My son, blessed are those who live abandoned to My Care, to My Protection, to My Will, for they shall have peace, joy, security. Theirs will be a fortune of wealth, a fortune of greater gifts, a fortune of rich pearls, for to be abandoned is

to have great faith, great trust, great confidence in the Father's Love. Peter, you must be a son that always lives in this state. You must know the benefits of living in this state, you must be one of the Father's children that He can love and hold and care for, one of His children that is confident, is sure, is positive that Daddy will care for him in all circumstances, in all situations, in all places, in all work you undertake for Him and as a part of your Earthly life. Peter, do you trust?, do you know?, do you believe that God loves you?!"

"Yes."

"Do you doubt that God is in complete control of everything?"

"No."

"Well, then, you have no excuse to not have faith, trust, and confidence in your loving Father. Peter, please don't hurt His Feelings by doubting Him in any way or for any reason! You must trust, you must be full of confidence, full of hope! Peter, you are now living in His Kingdom on Earth in a big way for He is in control of your life, your activities, your thoughts and with more denial by you of your will He will then be in complete control, for His Will will completely control you and then you will be shed of all this clothing of your human will, all of these rags of worry, doubting, evil desires, vices, weaknesses, so Peter, strip yourself of these dirty old rags and put on a white gown of precious linen, of Heavenly linen, a covering of God's Holy Will and you will be ready to meet Me in person, eye to eye, when I arrive shortly to claim My Kingdom, to hug My Children, to rule with an iron rod and an embrace of peace and love. Peter, I would like to whisper something in your ear, the words come from deep in My Heart. They are just words but their meaning is of great value. Listen, My son, listen to My Voice. 'My son, My Son of My Father's Will, My son of My Heart, my Son of My Mother's heart, My son full of My Spirit, I love you, I am in control of everything, I am going to care for your every need, I am always going to protect you.' Now Peter, please trust in My

Love which is the Father's Love for everything materially, spiritually and physically. Come, Peter, hold My Hand and that of My Mother, let us take you to a place of great peace, great joy, great contentment, it is Our House, Our House in Heaven. Peter, here in that room is where you will stay for all eternity after your stay on this Earth. Your stay here will be short, your room is all prepared, so Peter, please don't be all caught up in the world, be all caught up in love, Divine Love, the Love of Our Hearts. You have It, now use It, uncover It, let It flow from your being in all directions to all you meet in every conversation. Let It be seen in your eyes, your smile, let It be felt with your embrace, with your heavenly and holy kiss. My son, I love you with a love that is inconceivable, endless, infinite. Please don't hinder Me from embracing you, don't turn Me away with your own will where your self resides. Shed this part of you completely and fully and live suspended in the cloud, the light, the Divine Love of your Savior. My son, I mean what I have just said. I know they are just words but they are from My Heart, the Heart of your God, for I am One with the Trinity. So please son, please Peter, accept My Care, My Love, My Longing for your heart to be united to Mine in a bond that is perfect, in a bond that is homogeneous, a bond that is everlasting. Now, my son, you must return to your daily duties in this world. Do them for Me, for souls. I love you Peter."

"I love You, my All, thank You."

"You're welcome, please know that I mean every word that I have said and that these words are from My Heart."

"...THE LOST SHEEP NEED LOTS OF LOVE..." May 19, 1994 PM 11:00

"My son, I love you. Please take care to love each and every person that you come in contact with, for all are just as important to Me as you are and the lost sheep need lots of love, lots of Divine Love, to jar them out of the lethargy, out of their lukewarmness, their one-way trip. They are traveling

to Hell. My son, have My Peace, My Calmness, My Willingness to bend, to love and help so that love, Divine Love, will soften their hearts of stone into hearts that will receive the good news for time is running out and souls will be lost so love souls, love all souls. Peter, to be wrapped up in the world is to be headed down, down, down to the Netherworld, for if a soul is diverted by material wants and desires or pleasing creatures or stuck in the rut of vice, then this soul is dedicated to pleasing self, not loving God and doing His Will. So Peter, all of this will have to change to re-establish God's Purpose for mankind. Too many souls are being lost, for these traps set by the evil one are affecting all of My Children. The world is delivering them into his hands, the world is full of empty promises, full of unfulfilled desires, full of dead end streets. God the Father created the world for the creature to learn how to love and the world is teaching the creature how to hate. So all must change and it will. God's Will will be done. It must be. My son, after the changes are made, all will be renewed, all reborn and the harvest will be complete and the new Earth and new Heaven will be and all will live and do God's Holy, Divine, Glorious Will. All will be order, harmony and love will reign between all hearts. There will be peace, love, joy, for My Spirit will be poured out among all creatures. This is what awaits all those that persevere, all those that cut their ties to the world, all those that are striving to do God's Will, not their own, all those that are sincere in their heart to put God first and self interest last. So Peter, We are almost there, the storm must come, but it will end. So continue on your mission of love, to love and do God's Will and time will pass and one day you will wake up to Paradise, where all will have God's Will, live in God's Will and do God's Will. All will know the teachings and be focused on God above, not the world below. I love you Peter, My Son of My Divine Will."

"I love You, my Lord and my God."

"...LOVE ME BY LOVING OTHERS..." May 22, 1994 AM 07:30

"My son, I love you, carry your cross with joy, be at peace, love all those you are with, explode with joy, peace, love. My son, your mission continues, embrace it, love Me by loving others, help them smile, be of good cheer, time is short, souls, My son, souls. Continue, My son, We will have time later to write. My son, I will be with you all day today, I love you Peter."

"I love You, my King."

"LIVE ABANDONED TO MY CARE, TRUST IN MY LOVE..." May 22, 1994 PM 11:55

"My son, I love you. Live abandoned to My Care, trust in My Love, know of My Protection for you. My son, I need you to be of this state so your mission can be carried out. Peter, rest now, thank you for your efforts today to live in My Will. I love you, sleep in My Arms."

"I love You, my King."

"...INVOKE THE HELP AND SUPPORT AND PROTECTION OF THE HEAVENLY ANGELS" May 23, 1994 AM 06:00

"My dear child, this is your Mother. Jesus is my Lord and Savior, all praise, honor and glory be to the Holy Trinity! Peter, do you know how to stay in touch with heavenly beings? Unite yourself with their praises, with their worship of the Trinity. Be one with them in the Divine Will, for Angels, heavenly Angels only, do God's Will. Peter, the Angels are available to you to help you and protect you in this earthly pilgrimage. They have been given special anointing, special gifts to serve the creature in this capacity. You can call on them, you can ask them to come to your aid. St. Michael is a very powerful Archangel. He is fatal to the evil ones. St. Raphael and St. Gabriel have the special gifts also. My dear child, God the Father loves you and offers the support of the

Angels to all His children. Please accept it, use them, they desire to please the Father. Call on them, invoke them. My dear child, I love you. I am Queen of the Angels, you have my Heart, you are in the Army, my Army in these latter days. You are engaging with the enemy daily, so ask and you will receive help, support and protection. My dear Son of the Divine Will, continue to study the teachings of the Divine Will, blossom forth with love, peace, joy, let the Holy Spirit go, let Him inflame you each moment with Divine Love which indwells in your being, stay united to Our Hearts in every way, have no will of your own, deny self each day, hour, each moment and let the Divine Will reign in all of your being. Desire to please the Father, Son and Holy Spirit by your striving, your dedication, your perseverance, your endurance to become a child of God in all ways. Start your day now, your day of abandonment, your day of trust in the Father's Love, your day to love with His Love, your day to obey and be inspired to do God's Holy Will, your day to live moment by moment in a state of pure joy, peace, love, your day as a nothing in the Kingdom of God. My dear child, I love you and I will be helping you in all your efforts to do the Father's Will and if you invoke the help and support and protection of the heavenly Angels, you will receive their aid also. So begin now your mission for the day, go as a flame, go as a torch, go as a bright sun, go as a messenger of hope, I love you my child. "

"I love you, my Queen, my Mother, my Mom. "

"...GO FORTH ON THE ROAD THAT LEADS TO THE END OF THE RAINBOW" May 23, 1994 AM 10:30

"My son, yes, there are always too many things, too many work tasks, too many happenings in your earthly life to stay focused on loving your Lord. My son, this is why the teachings are so relevant to your life, for if you live the present moment and you don't concern yourself about past or future, about others, how they fit in or what you think they are thinking or will think, then your life becomes so simple and

your main occupation will be to love Me, to love others and to strive to live in and do God's Will and yes, My son, if you are letting God's Will truly reign in all of your activities and plans and provide the time and schedule, you will always have enough time for the activities in your life that are in accordance to God's Will to get done, to be completed. My son, you must be totally committed to living by the moment and desiring God's Will to reign fully every minute of your life, for if you are slipping in what you want to do, if you are trying to run the schedule, if you are depending on your plan to work, then you are interfering, you are full of contradictions, full of stress, full of worry, doubts and hence you are right back where you started in the maze of your human will. My son, you must step out of the maze, you must stay on the track, you must focus on the teachings and you must make them stick and become your life and then you will have complete peace, complete joy, complete order, complete harmony instead of the terrible mixture of your will and God's Will reigning. Peter, I want the best for you, I love you, I want you to love Me, so Peter, re-adjust, start anew, pick up the pieces and become a perfect Son of the Divine Will. Peter, you have My Grace, you have My Will, My Heart, My Mother's Heart, My Spirit so come back into My Arms and I will carry you and help you walk and go forth on the road that leads to the end of the rainbow. I love you, My son, keep your head up and your thoughts focused on love and the Father's Will."

"I love You, my Lord and my God."

"...LOVE WITH THE HEART OF GOD..." May 23, 1994 PM 08:00

"My son, to love without measure is to love with the Heart of God, to love without end is to love with the Heart of God, to love all creatures is to love with the Heart of God, to love without thoughts of self is to love with the Heart of God, to love with joy is to love with the Heart of God, to love without expecting repayment is to love with the Heart of God.

My son, God's Love is Divine, God's Love is one of a kind, God's Love is pure gold, God's Love is a treasure of endless value, God's Love is out of this world, God's Love is worth the sacrifice, God's Love is Heaven on Earth, God's Love is His Kingdom Come, God's Love is all yours, God's Love is given freely without any ties, without any obligations, without any payback required because God is Love and He loves you. Peter, you have His Spirit, you have His Love, give It, share It. This is your purpose, this is your goal, this is your life. Carry on, My son, with your mission of love. I love you Peter."

"I love You, my King of Love."

"...IF YOU HAVE NO WILL OF YOUR OWN YOUR BEING WILL BE VOID OF PRIDE AND SIN AND FULL OF THE LOVE OF GOD" May 24, 1994 PM 11:00

"My dear child, this is your Mother, I overflow with love for my Son, my Lord, the King of Kings, the Lord of Lords, Jesus Christ, my Lord, my Savior! Peter, my dear child, how love works, how love transforms and love becomes complete in a soul depends on the openness of the soul to the promptings of the Love of Christ, for a soul that is open without prior or hideous sin can receive love into his or her heart without resistance and the soul can then blossom forth in the Love of God, for God's Love desires hearts to dwell in, hearts where sin does not exist, hearts of purity. My dear child, be open to God's Holy Spirit of Love, be not closed to this great gift, for if a soul is full of pride, full of ego, full of self praise, God's Love can not come and dwell in the soul and if a soul is full of vice or sin of any type, love can not dwell in the soul. My dear child, you must stay humble and pure for love to reign. Expect not the Spirit of God, the Spirit of Love, God's Love, if the dwelling is full with no space in it for God's Love. Pride and sin are products of the human will. So, my son, cut the tree down and pull out the roots by ridding your being of your human will and you will be ridding all pride and

sin from your being and then the Love of God can be planted, can take root in the heart of the creature and grow and blossom, fill and occupy the being and love can triumph and overcome all evil in the life of the creature. So, my dear child, never let pride or sin into your life in even the smallest quantity, for the Love of God is too precious, too great a gift to lose, and if you have no will of your own your being will be void of pride and sin and full of the Love of God. Start the day, my son, and complete it without a will of your own, have only God's Will, let His Will reign in all your thoughts, words and actions and let love blossom from your being in every way to all creatures and stay in constant communion, in constant union with your God by being full of the Love of God and with this Love, love your God and you will be living the Triumph of my Immaculate Heart, you will be in union with all hearts, with the bond of everlasting love! I love you, my dear child."

"I love you, my Queen, my Mother, my Mommy."

"DO YOU KNOW WHY SHE IS BLESSED AMONG ALL WOMEN?...WELL, MY SON, IT IS HER HEART" May 24, 1994 AM 10:30

"My son, do you know why My Mother is so beautiful? Do you know why she is so honored? Do you know why she is blessed among all women? Do you know why she is full of grace? Well, My son, it is her Heart. Her Heart is full of the Love of God. She had no will of her own and her Heart was full of God's Holy Love, God's Holy Spirit. Her Heart is a flame of love, her Heart explodes with love. It is this love that is enclosed in My Mother's Heart and it is because she lives in the Divine Will that this precious Love of God enkindles the Love of God in all her children. God the Father created Mary as a perfect Mother for her Son, for His Body. He was born, He was raised, He was nourished with the love of her Heart. She always did God's Will and God's Love always flowed between Hearts, between her Heart and her Son's, between her Heart and the Father's. Her Heart is love without end, her

Heart is the Love of God, her Heart is pure without the stain of pride or sin, her Heart is a gift of God to us, her Heart is Immaculate and to be united to her Heart, to be one with her Heart is to be united to the Love of the Creator, the Love of God and the Triumph of the Immaculate Heart is the same as the Triumph of God's Love and God's Will is to establish love in all hearts of mankind and God's Will will be done - FIAT. I love you, My son, be united to My Mother's Heart, be united to My Heart, be united to the Spirit of God, be united to God's Love, for God's Love is one and the same, God's Love is one of a kind, God's Love will win and reign for ever and ever, amen. "

"Thank you My King of Love for Your Words of Love. "

"You're welcome, They are Truth, They are Life, They are Love. "

"...HAPPY ARE THOSE WHO LOVE WITHOUT MEASURE...THEY WILL LEARN QUICKLY THE TEACHINGS OF DIVINE WILL..." May 24, 1994 PM 05:40

"My son, happy are those who love without measure, they will be likened to My Saints in Heaven. They will learn quickly the teachings of Divine Will, for without doubt, a son or daughter who loves with the Love of God, who loves with their whole heart, is on the fast track in becoming a true Son or Daughter of the Father's Will. Peter, to love is to do the Father's Will, it is being a nothing, for to love you must put others first, you must not care about yourself but only about the creature you are helping or consoling or aiding in some way and when your whole life is given to loving the Creator and loving others you are totally detached from the world, from things, from creatures and to love is to be on fire with God's Holy Spirit and warm with gentleness and compassion. Peter, to love as your goal, to love as your purpose is to be focused on God's Design for your soul, for love is why you were created. Peter, don't be caught serving your own wants and desires. Serve others and I will love you, be caring and

providing for you, so when you are loving others you can be carefree and focused on the needs of others and know that the Father is well pleased. All of the circumstances and meetings you have now have been set up by the Father. They have been set up for you to love others with the Love of God, so know that you must always be ready to be a fireball of love wherever you are placed and as your days pass on this Earth you will grow quickly in the Love of God and the teachings of His Will. I love you, My Son of the Father's Will, go now to your meeting, go with the goal, the purpose, to inflame all those you meet, all those you come in contact with with the Love of God. "

"I love You, my Lord and Savior. "

"I AM THE QUEEN OF THE DIVINE WILL AND THESE WORDS ARE VERY IMPORTANT TO USHER IN THE NEW KINGDOM OF LOVE OF THE FATHER FOR THIS IS HIS WILL AND THE TIME IS NOW" May 25, 1994 AM 05:30

"My dear son, I love you, peace be with you. Jesus is my Lord and Savior, this is your Mother, have a beautiful day in the Kingdom of Love! Live each moment suspended in the cloud of light of the Divine Will, a cloud that encompasses you with God's Love, God's Protection, God's Care. My dear child, there is no way to be deceived about your mission of love, for all of the words that have been given to you have been given to instruct you in the lessons of loving your brothers and sisters and all the words given to instruct you in the teachings of having, living and doing the Father's Will are straight from the Trinity. They are without error, they have Our blessing, they have Our guidance in thought and word for yourself and all Our children who are striving to please the Trinity and do the Will of the Father. Peter, my dear child, you have done well to date processing the words, please don't let up, don't get slowed down for any reason. They need to be distributed as quickly as possible and this includes the second

book which will be complete soon, for these words are special, they will be used in a great way for teaching and informing my children of my Heart, of the Love of God and the way to love God by doing His Will always. Peter, I, your Mother, am your Mommy. I will personally take care of you each day of your life, I will guide you and protect you, you should have no fear of the evil one and when you are on your missions of love and are talking about and distributing these precious words, I will be with you personally. I will be imploring the Father with my prayers for the hearts to listen and respond with openness and acceptance to these special gifts, these Divine Words of Love and Guidance. Peter, I love you with all of my Heart. I know you feel unworthy of this but please know that it is true and my Heart is full of God's Love and even though you feel this way I feel differently than you for you are a child of God, you are my child, you are a brother of my Son, Jesus, my Lord, and this will always be, so Peter, feel secure that I am always with you to guide you and love you no matter what happens to you, no matter how big the cross is. It is not the Father's Will that I appear to you, at least now, so you must live with the promises of these words, that I am truly with you in all of your actions and activities of your life, so consult with me and depend on me to guide you and love you and know that God the Father has given me a more powerful position in His Kingdom than any other creature or spirit and that you may call on me for special needs you have in your walk and on your mission of love and your mission of distributing these words to the far reaches of the world and be sure, my dear child, that all those who join in this effort will receive a special place in the Kingdom of God and will also receive my care and protection in carrying out their part of the mission of distributing the words and implementing the teachings in their life's activities, for I am the Queen of the Divine Will and these words are important, very important, to usher in the new Kingdom of Love of the Father, for this is His Will and the time is now. So Peter, my dear child, rejoice to have been chosen for such a mission that will bring joy to the Father, Son and Holy Spirit as you complete it. Have no confidence in yourself to complete it. Trust in Us and it will happen for God's Will will be done - FIAT! Peter, I love you with the boundless Love of the Trinity, I embrace you, I give you a holy kiss, live in wonderment, in joy, in peace about your mission, don't try to comprehend it or try to understand why you have been chosen for it, just live moment by moment loving your God, loving others and being obedient to the inspirations you receive to do and act in all the happenings of your life, all the activities of your life, all the duties of your mission of this work. Go now Peter, begin the day and remember; love, love, love and live the moment!"

"I love you, my dear precious Mother and Mommy."

"...BECOME A TRUE IMITATOR OF JESUS CHRIST IN EVERY WAY AT ALL TIMES IF YOU JUST GET RID OF YOUR WILL AND LIVE IN THE WILL OF GOD" May 25, 1994 PM 07:15

"My dear child, I love you! Do you know who is the greatest person that ever lived, the greatest Christian, the person completely full of the Will of God and the Spirit of God? Well, of course it was my Lord and Savior, King of Kings, Lord of Lords, my Son, Jesus Christ! Peter, to live in the Will of God is to be one with the King of Kings, for Jesus is God-man and His Will is the Father's Will and to be united to God's Love is to be united to Jesus. He is your ideal, your model, your loving brother, your King, your Savior. He always did the Father's Will because He had the Father's Will and now you have the Father's Will and if you live in the Will then the Will of Jesus will act and reign in you as long as you rid your being of your own will. So Peter, you can become a true imitator of Jesus Christ in every way at all times if you just get rid of your will and live in the Will of God! It's that simple and of course, if the Will of Jesus is reigning in your life you will always do the perfect, just and glorious Will of the

Father as Christ always did while He was in the flesh on this Earth in His Private and Public Life. Peter, isn't this the ultimate goal of all Christians? Well, the key to the obtaining of this goal is to kill and rid your being of your own will and with these teachings fully implemented in your life you will live at all times in the Will of God and now all will be Jesus' in every way and all will live in love, in order, in constant helping and caring for one another, all will be Christ to each other, love will reign between hearts, pure love, the Love of Jesus, now can come the Kingdom of Love established on Earth and now all will do God's Will at all times. It will be Heaven here on Earth! My dear child, soon, soon, will the Love of God, the Will of God reign in the hearts of all mankind. My dear child, no one can stop this from occurring, no government, no nation, for God's Will will reign!"

"Alleluia, come Lord Jesus!"

"Relax, my son. Peter, live in His Will and enjoy life in His Will, life with peace and joy, life without cares or troubles, life as the Father designs for you, life in union with the Father, life in union with all creation, life of pure ecstasy! This life with these gifts is for you, free of charge! The Father presents it to you to give you a present, a gift of His Love. Love Him in return with the Love of His Heart, this is all He asks, all He desires from you. Peter, now is the time to perfect the teachings, so keep it up, don't slacken and you will have the most precious gift God can give you, life without end living in the Kingdom of Love, Joy, Peace. I love you my child."

"I love you, my Queen, my Mother, my Mom."

"...IT WILL BE A GLORIOUS DAY...THE KINGDOM OF LOVE, THE KINGDOM OF GOD, THE KINGDOM OF THE DIVINE WILL WILL BE ESTABLISHED AND REIGN FOREVER ON EARTH AS IT IS IN HEAVEN!" May 25, 1994 PM 10:20

"How blessed are the true Sons and Daughters of the

Father's Will! Theirs is Paradise on Earth, theirs is peace without end, theirs is joy without end, theirs is a life of the Divine, a life of the Family of God, a life of the envy of all! Oh how blessed are the fortunate ones, the choice ones, the great ones who rid their being of the old, the dying, the selfish human will and obtain the everlasting and eternal, the glorious and almighty Divine Will of the Father and when the day comes, the night ends, the dawn arises, there will be the faithful Sons and Daughters of the King of Kings, the Lord of Lords, the First and the Last of all of creation to rise up and meet, rise up and greet, rise up and rejoice, rise up and sing 'Glory to God in the Highest, Glory to God the Almighty, Glory to God the Father' and peace, love and joy to all those who love, all those who have, all those who live, all those who do, the Will, the Divine Will of the Father! Oh what a joy it will be to be united in the Holy Will of the Father, to be of one mind, one spirit, one body of believers that will carry the banner 'HIS KINGDOM COME, HIS WILL BE DONE FOREVER AND EVER AND EVER AMEN AMEN AMEN' and We will walk and We will talk and We will love as one body united, one body joined, one Body of Christ. Yes, My son, it will be a glorious day, all of Heaven will be present and will rejoice, for the Kingdom of Love, the Kingdom of God, the Kingdom of the Divine Will will be established and reign forever on Earth as it is in Heaven! Praised be the Father's Will, praised be the Father's Love! Peter, the future, the hope, the joy of the Father's Plan be yours! I love you, My Son of the Divine Will."

"I love You, my King and thank you."

"You're welcome, live the moment and stay at peace in the Kingdom of God."

"...SPREAD THE GOOD NEWS OF THE KINGDOM COMING ON EARTH AS IT IS IN HEAVEN!" May 26, 1994 AM 05:40

"My son, how blessed are all those who strive to live in

the Will of the Father, for theirs shall be a Heaven on Earth without end and blessed are those who desire to please the Father by doing His Will at all times for their efforts will receive great rewards and blessed are those who desire to please the Trinity with their heart's intentions, their actions of love that come from their desires to love others, to love their God! Oh how blessed are My Children of My Will, Oh how I love them without measure, without end, without reserve, for they desire only to please their God with all they say, all they think, all they do! I embrace them and hold them on My Bosom close to My Heart! They are My Faithful Children of great sanctity, for I shall pour out My Gifts upon them, I shall guard and protect them, I shall guide and direct them and they shall be rich with My Blessings, they shall receive My Special Care, My Fatherly Care and no one shall be allowed to touch them physically or spiritually, for My Divine Light will enclose them in My Love! Oh My son, I want a large family of Children of My Will, a family too large to count, so spread the Words from My Heart that My children will know the path to the Father's House where their Daddy awaits them with open arms and their Brother longs for their company and their Mother wants to love and caress them and dress them with gowns of white linen! Oh My son, go forth into the desert, into the wastelands, into the dark cities and gloomy abodes and spread the Words, the Words from My Heart and as they receive these heavenly Words their lives will become Divine, their love will become Divine and their hearts will transform into hearts of purity and their wills they will leave behind and they will be filled with the fire of Divine Love and they will receive the Divine Will of the Father and the deserts, the wastelands, the dark cities, the gloomy abodes will become a new Heaven, totally reborn, totally renewed, totally transformed into a Paradise of Love, a Kingdom of Love that will last forevermore!! So be it, for My Will will be done - FIAT!!! Go now, My son, continue on your mission to love and spread the good news of the Kingdom coming on Earth as

it is in Heaven! I love you Peter."
"I love You, my Lord and God."

The printing and distribution of this book is dependent on your help and collaboration. Additional copies are available from;

Triumph Books and Media
P.O. Box 10374
Sarasota, Florida 34278

Books Available:

1. "Triumph of Love" (Messages, January - March 1994)
2. "His Kingdom Come, His Will Be Done" (Messages, April - May 1994)

$2.00 each
Bulk pricing available on request

Please enclose $2.00 + 10% of order for shipping and handling and 7% sales tax.

APPENDIX A

Another member of the Sarasota Prayer Group was given a message as follows that confirmed Peter's messages were from Jesus. This message was given to Ken Hipps on January 11, 1994. This message was not requested and Ken did not know that I had started to receive messages as of January 2, 1994.

"...My son, tell Peter he indeed hears My Voice speaking to his heart. Tell him it gladdens My Heart every time he sits in front of Me in surrender, tell him I love him and to grasp onto the words and to live the words I pour into his heart. I will truly guide him on a new journey of love. Tell him not to fear this new journey, but to embrace it. I will spell out this new journey very clearly. It is time now for him to act. His grooming is over, he has tasted the fruits of My Love. Tell him, it is only the smallest of samples that he has tasted, that the fullness of the banquet that lays ahead is beyond his imagination. Tell him now to embrace it, to find fullness in it, to find peace in it, by surrender, by obedience, by listening quietly to My Heart speaking to his, then responding, with no fear."

THE SORROWFUL MYSTERIES OF THE ROSARY
April 15, 1994 AM

THE AGONY IN THE GARDEN "My son, contemplate the loneliness of My Being, the sorrow I suffered, for I was deserted by all except a few during My Passion and I foresaw My Passion on this night before Me, every detail, and I suffered from a troubled heart, for I foresaw all the sinners that would not accept My Love and take advantage of My Sacrifice. My Son, I literally sweat blood, I was so troubled and full of agony for all those sinners who had stubborn wills and would therefore allow the evil one full rein in them and would suffer eternally in the abyss. These sinners would not accept My Love, My Care, My Gift of Eternal Life. Oh what sorrow, Oh what agony I suffered!"

THE SCOURGING AT THE PILLAR "The whips, My son, the whips, they struck so hard, such impact, such pain resulted and it did not end. It tore out pieces of My Flesh everywhere, even My Face. My son, the blood flowed down My Body like water, it was so plentiful and the blood splattered on the onlookers, including My Mother. Her face was so sorrowful, I was tied so tight to the column that My Skin tore open, all of this for love of mankind."

THE CROWNING WITH THORNS "There I sat and they put this crown of long, sharp thorns on My Head. They pounded it on. It drove the thorns into My Head. It was all to mock Me for they did not believe that I was the King of all. The blood poured out in streams into My Eyes and Ears and Mouth, all of this for love of creatures."

THE CARRYING OF THE CROSS "The weight of the cross was great, for My Body was weak. I carried it with love for it was the symbol that I would be thought of for all eternity. It was the purpose of My being there, the salvation of souls. Carry your crosses, My son, carry them joyfully with peace. Unite them to Mine. The falls were bleak, they were so crushing, but I got up with hope that others would follow My

Example. Thank you, My son, for your desire to follow Me and love Me by your willingness to carry your many crosses."

THE CRUCIFIXION "They nailed Me to the cross. They stretched and pulled My Arms, they put their foot on My Forearm and drove the nails right through My Flesh and Bones. What pain! And then they raised Me up and dropped the cross with Me in the hole, slamming Me and shocking My Body. What treatment, what pain, and I hung there in the cold with the flies, with the mocking, with the onlookers making a point out of Me being overpowered by humans and that I must not therefore be God, all for love, My son, all for love."

AUTHORITY OF THE CHURCH

According to a decree of the Congregation for the Doctrine of Faith, approved by H.H. Pope Paul VI, (1966), it is now permitted to publish and distribute without an Imprimatur books about new apparitions, revelations, prophecies, or miracles. In accordance with the regulations of the Second Vatican Council, we who publish and distribute this book state that we do not wish to precede the judgement of the Church in this matter, to whose authority we humbly and obediently submit.

With reference to private revelations, H.H. Pope Urban VIII, 1623-44 has stated:

"In cases which concern private revelations, it is better to believe than not to believe, for, if you believe, and it is proven true, you will be happy that you have believed, because our Holy Mother asked it. If you believe, and it should be proven false, you will receive all blessings as if it had been true, because you believed it to be true."

NOTE: The messages in this book are recorded as they were received. Where titles exist for messages, they are the work of

Peter, attempting to best give the key point of the message following by taking a selected quote from it. These messages were received by Peter beginning in January of 1994. All Biblical references are taken from the Douay-Rheims Bible.

"Extinguish not the spirit. Despise not prophecies. But Prove all things; hold fast that which is good. From all appearance of evil refrain yourselves." (1 Thessalonians 5:19-22)

"It shall come to pass in the last days, (saith the Lord), I will pour out of my Spirit upon all flesh: and your sons and your daughters shall prophesy, and your young men shall see visions, and your old men shall dream dreams. And upon my servants indeed, and upon my handmaids will I pour out in those days of my spirit, and they shall prophesy." (Acts 2:17-18)

INDEX

04/03, 1994 AM 06:00 "...you will not die but live eternally" *13*

04/03, 1994 PM 11:45 "...don't be...slave to material wants." *13*

04/04, 1994 AM 06:45 "...reflect the light of the 'Son'" *15*

04/04, 1994 PM 01:00 "...be realistic and future minded" *15*

04/04, 1994 PM 11:00 "...be united to God's Will!" . . . *16*

04/05, 1994 AM 06:10 "...live in His Will and have peace..." *19*

04/05, 1994 PM 01:30 "...the plane of the Divine Will..." *19*

04/05, 1994 PM 10:15 "...take time out...to pray..." . . *20*

04/06, 1994 AM 05:30 "...strive for the finish line..." . . *21*

04/07, 1994 AM 00:15 "...care not about yourself so I can..." *21*

04/07, 1994 AM 10:15 "...live in..do My Will moment by moment" *22*

04/08, 1994 AM 06:45 "...Satan...wants to upset your life..." *23*

04/08, 1994 PM 00:00 "...Love is the Kingdom of God" *23*

04/08, 1994 PM 11:00 "...the fulfillment of My Prayer..." *24*

04/09, 1994 PM 10:15 "..I want to talk..about My Love for you" *25*

04/10, 1994 AM 11:00 "...this is the day of mercy..." . . *27*

04/10, 1994 PM 11:20 "I need your prayers and all..children's" *28*

04/11, 1994 AM 06:15 "...live and practice the...teachings.." *29*

04/11, 1994 PM 02:30 "...to live in and to do His Will are..." *30*

04/11, 1994 PM 11:40 "...The Divine Will will be established." 32

04/12, 1994 AM 10:15 "...The Garden of the Divine Will..." 33

04/12, 1994 PM 11:15 "...living in God's Will..will be..love." 34

04/13, 1994 AM 05:50 "...My Will..he stop drinking completely" 35

04/14, 1994 AM 01:00 "..stay abandoned in..Will of the Father" 36

04/14, 1994 AM 06:00 "..My Will is having all of these traits" 37

04/14, 1994 AM 12:00 "a son or daughter..must.fulfill..duties" 38

04/14, 1994 PM 10:00 "...you are united to the Trinity..." 39

04/15, 1994 PM 01:20 "Be a meek and humble lamb..never.angry." 40

04/15, 1994 PM 11:00 "...you will be taken care of" . . 41

04/16, 1994 AM 05:35 "..living in His Will is the best.." 41

04/17, 1994 PM 03:15 "..full of the Wisdom of.Divine Will" 45

04/17, 1994 PM 12:30 "...live in the present moment" 44

04/18, 1994 AM 08:00 "Have this peace so.you.live in My Will" 46

04/18, 1994 AM 09:20 "I want a perfect relationship with you" 46

04/18, 1994 PM 10:00 "..Mary's place in the Plan of Salvation" 47

04/19, 1994 AM 06:00 "...have you begun to realize what is.." 49

04/19, 1994 PM 01:15 "step back from the world by..." 50

04/19, 1994 PM 10:20 "...sleep is a gift of love

from.Father" *50*

04/20, 1994 AM 05:30 "...strive to live moment by moment" *50*

04/20, 1994 PM 07:40 "..be one with My Spirit for My Spirit.." *51*

04/21, 1994 AM 06:10 "Turn over everything to Me, ask for..." *52*

04/21, 1994 AM 12:00 "My son, come home..." *53*

04/21, 1994 PM 09:50 ".holiness is to do My Will at all times" *54*

04/22, 1994 AM 05:30 "..I will press you into a diamond and I" *55*

04/22, 1994 PM 06:10 "...don't put up any road blocks to Me.." *56*

04/22, 1994 PM 10:40 "Tell her she is My Little Flower..." *57*

04/22, 1994 PM 11:40 "The Love of God is Power" . . . *57*

04/23, 1994 AM 06:45 "...live each moment loving all" *57*

04/23, 1994 PM 09:40 "..only entertain these thoughts..." *58*

04/24, 1994 AM 06:00 "..My Heart is a..source of gifts from." *59*

04/24, 1994 PM 00:05 "..love is the mountain, evil is..." *60*

04/25, 1994 AM 06:45 "Do you not trust Me? Do you not think." *61*

04/25, 1994 PM 02:00 "..be transformed into a Dove of Peace" *62*

04/26, 1994 AM 00:05 ".family life is the future of the Earth" *64*

04/26, 1994 AM 06:10 "The Triumph of my Immaculate Conception" *64*

04/26, 1994 AM 08:45 "My child, be filled with grace..." *65*

04/27, 1994 PM 10:00 "...only do God's Will..." *68*

04/28, 1994 AM 05:45 "...how to please the Father..." *69*

04/28, 1994 AM 08:45 "Join the army that will be victorious" *70*

04/29, 1994 AM 00:45 "..trusting in money is an insult to God" *73*

04/29, 1994 AM 01:00 "I will give you strength to make up for" *71*

04/29, 1994 PM 11:00 "Now is the time that this book is..open" *71*

04/30, 1994 AM 06:30 "..I will be your Mother of your dreams." *74*

05/01, 1994 AM 03:00 "...a summary" *75*

05/01, 1994 AM 11:45 "...not to be concerned about the future" *76*

05/01, 1994 PM 11:50 "..it is important to get them out.do it" *78*

05/02, 1994 AM 06:00 "The day is made up of short segments.." *78*

05/02, 1994 AM 11:00 "Hallelujah...the end of the rainbow!" *79*

05/02, 1994 PM 11:00 "The key is to have His Will reign.." *80*

05/03, 1994 AM 06:00 "Ask to be inspired at every segment.." *81*

05/03, 1994 AM 10:00 "..unite your prayers and actions..." *82*

05/03, 1994 PM 11:30 "..I love you and wish...a mission.." *83*

05/04, 1994 AM 06:00 "...I will be you..." *84*

05/04, 1994 PM 03:45 "...living in My Will..number one.." *85*

05/04, 1994 PM 06:30 "...love Me with your all..." ... *85*

05/04, 1994 PM 09:00 "..how do you control your thoughts.." *86*

05/05, 1994 AM 06:00 "..all the remnant flock will

become.." *87*

05/05, 1994 AM 11:30 "..love Us with..your new Will.." *88*

05/05, 1994 PM 05:30 "..you must be aware of your thoughts.." *89*

05/05, 1994 PM 11:30 "...to always do God's Will..." *89*

05/06, 1994 AM 06:00 "..you must be a gardener of love.." *90*

05/08, 1994 AM 00:45 "..thank you for letting me use you" *91*

05/08, 1994 AM 06:00 ".live today and every day in the moment" *91*

05/08, 1994 PM 05:00 ".use these keys to open up the.doors." *92*

05/09, 1994 AM 05:45 ".you must be reborn in the Divine Will" *93*

05/09, 1994 AM 08:45 "...I will inspire you..." *94*

05/09, 1994 AM 11:00 "...The Triumph of Love.union of.hearts." *94*

05/09, 1994 PM 11:45 "..straight 'A' student.of.Divine Will" *95*

05/10, 1994 AM 06:00 "..one hundred and ten percent committed" *96*

05/10, 1994 AM 11:30 "...always be truthful..." *99*

05/10, 1994 PM 01:00 "...teaching you to live in My Will" *97*

05/10, 1994 PM 07:45 "..when men's hearts are changed..." *100*

05/11, 1994 AM 05:45 "..have a beautiful day..in Our Will" *102*

05/13, 1994 AM 06:00 "Peter, you are a messenger of hope.." *102*

05/13, 1994 PM 00:30 "These words are spirit and life,..." *103*

05/13, 1994 PM 11:30 "You must be a little child..." . *104*

05/14, 1994 PM 02:00 "..my children must have hope in.future." 106

05/14, 1994 PM 11:00 "The new Era..a new Earth, a new Heaven." 107

05/15, 1994 AM 06:00 "Have a beautiful day in the Kingdom!" 108

05/15, 1994 PM 02:00 "realize the power you have now..." 109

05/15, 1994 PM 11:30 "..walk closer and closer to me each day" 110

05/16, 1994 AM 11:00 "..if it were not for this mission.." 111

05/16, 1994 PM 10:00 "..You must be focused on God's Will" 112

05/17, 1994 PM 05:00 "place the book in the hands.my.children" 113

05/17, 1994 PM 11:00 "My Spirit is the life of your being" 114

05/18, 1994 PM 09:00 "have hope.without hope all seems lost" 116

05/19, 1994 AM 11:00 "Trust in My Love...for everything.." 117

05/19, 1994 PM 11:00 "..the lost sheep need lots of love.." 119

05/22, 1994 AM 07:30 "..love Me by loving others.." . 121

05/22, 1994 PM 11:55 "Live abandoned to My Care, trust.." 121

05/23, 1994 AM 06:00 "..invoke the..heavenly Angels.." 121

05/23, 1994 AM 10:30 "..go..to the end of the rainbow" 122

05/23, 1994 PM 08:00 "..love with the Heart of God.." 123

05/24, 1994 AM 10:30 "Do you know why she is blessed...?" 125

05/24, 1994 PM 05:40 "happy are those who love

         w/out measure" *126*

05/24, 1994 PM 11:00 "..if you have no will of your
         own.." *124*

05/25, 1994 AM 05:30 "I am the Queen of the Divine
         Will.." *127*

05/25, 1994 PM 07:15 ".become a true imitator of
         Jesus Christ" *129*

05/25, 1994 PM 10:20 "..It will be a glorious day.." . *130*

05/26, 1994 AM 05:40 "..spread the good news of the
         Kingdom." *131*

CONCORDANCE

a nothing 1,8,18,26,35,40,46,53,55,56,71, 72, 75,
76, 82, 84, 85, 89, 90, 94, 96, 111, 113,
122, 126

a special place 128

abandoned to My Care 117, 121

abandonment . 15, 22, 30, 36, 39, 62, 69, 75, 87, 91, 101,
117, 122

abyss 38, 61, 136

accept My Care 119

Act of Abandonment 69, 75, 87

Act of Humility 46, 75, 87

Act of Love 28, 44, 54, 69, 75, 86

add 31, 75

adventure 103, 112

adventure of love 112

agitated 68

agitation 65

all must change 120

all seems lost 116

all to Himself 117

almost there 120

alone 58, 83

Alpha and Omega 62

always be truthful 99, 100

anchor 49, 80

anchors 14

Angels . . . 21, 53, 55, 68, 82, 83, 86, 102, 109, 121, 122

angry 23, 40, 112

anointing 63, 121

anticipation 10

anxiety 17, 22, 26, 38, 97, 99

anything 13, 19, 27, 39, 43, 45, 51, 72, 81, 98

Apostle of My Love 1, 72

Apostles of the Last Days 1, 72

apple *106*
Army of Christ 70
army of devils 68
Army of Love 70
attachment 63
attentive 66
attitude 30, 76, 94, 106
awe 72
awesome 9, 50, 80
bear 29
beautiful 13, 33, 60, 85, 102, 108, 109, 125, 127
being . . . 8,14,16,18, 19, 22-25, 28, 30, 32, 35-37, 39-42,
                     45-47, 49-51, 55-59, 65, 67, 69-71, 75,
                     79-81, 83, 86, 89, 93, 95, 96, 98, 99, 101,
                     106-108, 110, 111, 114, 115, 119, 120, 122,
                     124-126, 129-131, 136, 137
bicker 65
big brother 91
Bingo 108
bird soars 85
birth pains 70
blessing 30, 38, 48, 127
blind faith 105
blinded 16
boast 65
bodily functions 71
bond of love 35, 105, 106
book . . 1,7,8,45, 46, 58, 70-72, 104, 106, 113, 128, 134,
                                                             137
burn 55, 104, 109
business 7
calm will ensue 116
calmness 46, 63, 116, 120
care . . . 13,15,17,19-23,26, 36-38, 40, 41, 45-47, 49, 51,
                     52, 62, 66, 70, 73, 74, 77, 82, 86, 91, 92,
                     95, 96, 105, 108, 109, 111, 114, 116-119,

                             121, 126-128, 132, 136

carefree *43, 127*
carnal love *114*
carry your cross *44, 97, 121*
casualties *67*
catalyst *67*
chained *33, 65, 88, 103*
change your habits *93, 111*
changes He desires *1, 100*
chaos *17, 24, 61*
character *37*
cherish *65*
child of God *42, 49, 59, 67, 106, 116, 122, 128*
child's innocence *105*
children . . *1, 9, 13-16, 18, 20, 21, 25, 26, 28-30, 32, 34,*
                  38, 41, 43, 45, 47, 48, 58, 59, 62, 64, 65,
                  67, 72, 78, 80, 83, 84, 87, 88, 90, 93, 98,
              102-104, 106, 108, 110, 113, 114, 116-118,
                  120, 122, 125, 127, 128, 132
choke them *86*
Christ *5,7,8,31,40,42,60-65, 67, 68, 70-72, 95, 117,*
                        124, 129, 130, 131
Christian *8, 48, 71, 72, 129*
circumstances . . *19, 22, 36, 40, 83, 89, 90, 97, 118, 127*
claim My Kingdom *118*
clay *57, 67*
clean that desk *107*
clearly marked *68*
close the window *68*
cloud of light *127*
clouds *55, 112*
combined resources *83*
comfort My Children *102*
command *39*
company *132*
complete transformation *80, 108*

149

complicated *68*
confession *7, 35*
confidence *22, 26, 30, 110, 118, 129*
confusion *17, 22, 24, 80, 99, 106, 111*
conquer *28, 41, 61, 88*
consecrated *7, 31, 39, 47, 54, 67, 71, 83, 84, 87*
consecration . *26, 39, 40, 42, 44, 59, 67, 69, 75, 79, 110*
console *28, 29, 95*
constant *49, 55, 69, 77, 96, 101, 111, 125, 130*
constant drag *111*
consult *128*
contained *31*
control . . *13, 17, 19, 22-24, 37, 38, 42-44, 51, 77, 86-89,*
92, 93, 97, 98, 101-103, 106, 110, 114,
116-118
conversion *67, 68, 111, 115*
conversion process *115*
Crack *67, 83, 109*
created . . . *1, 29, 34, 59, 61, 85, 100, 114, 120, 125, 126*
Creator . . *17, 29, 31, 34, 37, 42, 57, 63, 80, 85, 89, 97,*
102, 117, 126
creatures . *1, 8, 10, 14, 16-18, 20-24, 30, 34, 35, 37, 40,*
42-45, 48, 49, 54, 55, 61, 63, 65, 79, 80,
85, 92, 98, 100, 102, 103, 113, 114, 120,
123, 125, 126, 136
cross . . . *21, 29, 40, 44, 97, 98, 101, 121, 128, 136, 137*
cross removed *98*
crosses *45, 51, 55, 64, 76, 84, 112, 136, 137*
crown with stars *97*
crush *48*
current *19, 36, 53, 107*
Daddy awaits them *132*
dead end path *66*
dead end streets *120*
deception *34, 61, 99*
deception is straight from Hell *99*

defined *17, 40, 95*

demons *64*

Design of God *108*

detached *20, 79, 97, 106, 126*

detached from everything *106*

detail *22, 62, 98, 101, 112, 136*

devil *23, 28, 31, 77, 97*

devils *33, 68*

die *13, 24, 42, 48, 67, 107*

die to the world *67*

dirty old rags *118*

disasters *116*

disorder *24, 61*

dissension *61*

distribute this book *113, 137*

Divine Commands *86*

Divine Fire *84*

Divine Formula *67, 68*

Divine Light *79, 97, 132*

Divine Providence *44, 77, 102*

Divine Will *1, 7-10, 16, 19, 20, 24-27, 29-34, 38-40,
42-46, 48, 54, 58, 59, 60, 68, 69, 72-75,
77-89, 92-98, 101, 103, 106, 110, 111, 120,
121-123, 125-128, 130-132*

domestic family *64*

don't get gloomy *117*

don't hinder Me *119*

don't hurt His Feelings *118*

don't slacken *130*

doubt *9, 19, 46, 51, 68, 93, 104, 118, 126*

doubts *102, 123*

Dove of Peace *62, 63*

drowned *24, 52, 61, 109*

dumfoundness *72*

duties *38, 46, 47, 50, 51, 85, 107, 119, 129*

dwell *21,23,34,47,52,54,59, 62, 63, 68, 70, 82, 95,*

103, 124

eagle gliding *63*
Earth *1,8,10,16,19,21,22, 24-26, 32, 33, 37, 38, 42,*
43, 49, 51, 60, 62, 64, 71, 72, 79, 81-83,
87-89, 96, 100, 101, 103, 104, 107, 108,
114, 118-120, 124, 127, 130-132
earthly mother *29*
ecstasy *72, 130*
ego *14, 77, 124*
ejaculatory prayers *75, 86, 92, 102*
electrocutes others *96*
eleventh hour *67*
embrace . . . *26, 34, 41, 51, 53, 60, 62, 70, 86, 103, 107,*
112, 118, 119, 121, 129, 132, 135
empty *18, 45, 52, 115, 120*
end of the rainbow . . . *10,48,60,79,80,106,108, 113, 122,*
123
endurance *122*
endure *57*
engineer *7*
enmity *108*
enslaved *67*
environment *65*
Era *1,7,9,16,25,31,33-35,37, 41, 44, 49, 58, 61, 65,*
72, 73, 88, 100, 101, 107, 108, 114
Era of the Divine Will *1, 72*
Eternal Bliss *21, 79*
eternal bond *105*
eternal gaze *88, 108*
eternity . . . *10,16,37,54,66,79, 80, 96, 97, 114, 119, 136*
everlasting bond *106*
evil *13,14,24,25,27,28,33,36,41, 45, 47, 49, 54, 56,*
58, 59, 60, 61, 64, 65, 67-70, 77, 84, 87,
90, 92, 93, 97, 99, 100, 103-105, 108, 111,
115, 116, 118, 120, 121, 125, 128, 136, 138
evil pleasures *97*

example *8, 14, 15, 39, 79, 101, 137*
exciting *24*
expectation *33*
experience *17, 51, 60, 66, 84*
explode *28, 83, 85, 112, 121*
explode with joy *121*
faculties *38, 69*
Fall asleep *29, 32*
false security *117*
family . . *8, 14, 16, 24, 25, 28, 29, 36, 38, 41, 43, 47-49,*
64, 69, 71, 80, 86, 88, 90, 94-96, 102,
105-107, 111, 116, 117, 131, 132
family life *28, 64*
fast track *126*
fatal to the evil ones *121*
Father's Kingdom *68*
Father's Wrath *69, 87, 100, 110, 116*
fervor *10*
Fiat . . . *17,25,26,29,30,32, 33, 37, 42-44, 48, 60, 66, 70,*
88, 95, 102, 112, 117, 126, 129, 132
fight *65*
filled with grace *65, 66*
filth *65*
financial *51, 98*
finish *21, 97*
fireball *127*
fireball of love *127*
First and the Last *17, 131*
float *36*
flow *35, 63, 91, 107, 119*
flowers of love *73, 108*
focus *64, 73, 75, 90, 93, 95, 123*
focused . . *21, 32, 38, 47, 50, 68, 69, 75, 87, 90, 92, 97,*
102, 112, 113, 120, 122, 123, 126, 127
focused on love *123*
follower *68, 71*

forehead 87
forest 17, 86
forever and ever 131
fortune of wealth 117
foundation 28, 61, 81, 97
free of charge 130
freedom will begin 108
friend 52, 73, 94, 109
fruit 64, 80
full battle array 68
full of contradictions 123
full of grace 65, 66, 125
full of pride 99, 112, 124
future . . . 1,7,8,13,15-17, 22, 25, 27, 30, 33, 42, 44, 45,
47, 49, 50, 51, 58, 62, 64, 65, 76-79, 87,
88, 96-98, 100-103, 106, 108, 109, 117,
122, 131
future is bright 117
gain the momentum 104
garden . . . 1, 33, 34, 46, 53, 60, 65, 72, 73, 91, 108, 136
garden is the world 91
garden of Paradise 73
garden of purity 108
gardener of love 90, 91
gate 68, 108
General of Love 68
gently teaching 98
get them out 78
gift of God 9, 126
gift of love 50, 94
glorious day 130, 131
glue 80
go forth 122, 123, 132
God is in control 17, 19, 110, 116
God of Abraham 100
God's Holy Will . . 25, 31, 32, 39, 42, 48, 49, 54, 62, 63,

71, 72, 75-77, 79, 81, 82, 87, 88, 93, 96,
97, 105, 106, 110, 118, 122

God's Will will reign *54, 112, 130*

going to Heaven *72*

gold of love *109*

Gospel *14, 15, 20, 31, 73, 76*

gowns of white linen *132*

grace . . . *29, 31, 35, 43, 57, 59, 65, 66, 68, 93, 97, 105,*
108, 123, 125

grain of sand *60, 73*

grand schemes *88*

grasp *8, 29, 45, 50, 59, 135*

great apostasy *111*

great graces *101*

great responsibility *101*

great sanctity *132*

greatest person *129*

grow . . *27, 32, 44, 58, 63, 66, 69, 76, 83, 86, 87, 90, 91,*
104, 106, 107, 125, 127

growth *23, 29, 36, 59, 64, 66, 81, 83, 91, 105, 111*

guide . . . *19, 23, 29, 48, 52, 59, 66, 69, 74, 78, 91, 101,*
106, 107, 111, 128, 132, 135

gullible faith *105*

Hallelujah *79, 80, 95*

handle *61, 62*

happy . . . *13,15,21,23,38,40, 43, 48, 62, 71, 79, 86, 96,*
97, 104, 105, 107, 114, 126, 137

hard rock *67*

hardened and rebelling children *93*

harmony . . . *1, 17, 22, 36, 37, 41, 60, 61, 100, 103, 109,*
120, 123

harshness *65*

harvest *120*

have His Love *124*

have His Spirit *116, 124*

He owns all *117*

health 79
heart beating 98
Heart of Love 72
Heart of the Queen 108
heart that smells 92
hearts of purity 124, 132
hearts of stone 67, 85, 120
heaven . . . 1, 5, 8, 14, 19, 26, 29, 31, 32, 48, 51, 60, 66,
        71-73, 79, 82, 83, 86, 88, 96, 100, 101,
        103, 107-109, 111, 112, 119, 120, 124, 126,
                                           130-133
Heaven here on Earth 130
Heaven on Earth 19, 60, 108, 124, 132
heavenly Angels 121, 122
heavenly beings 121
heavy cross 101
help . . . 7,18,23,28,50,53,55, 56, 61, 68, 69, 75, 81, 87,
        90, 95, 107, 113, 120-123, 134
her Heart is pure 126
hideous sin 124
His Embrace 103
His Fiat 29
His Pure Will 81
His Will be done 3, 37, 66, 131, 134
His Will will rule 16, 107
hit the target 72
hold My Hand 119
holiness 21, 23, 30, 36, 54, 59, 66
holy . . . 7,9,17-19,21,24-26,29-32, 35, 37, 39, 40, 42-44,
        46-49, 51-54, 60, 62, 63, 66, 68, 69, 71-79,
        81, 82, 84, 86, 87, 88-90, 92-94, 96, 97,
        102, 103, 105-110, 113, 114, 116, 118,
        119-122, 124-126, 129, 131, 137
Holy Catholic Faith 76
hope 1,7,13,25,27,30,45,51,53, 65, 70, 78, 88, 100,
        102, 103, 106, 108, 109, 113, 116-118, 122,

131, 136
hopeless and depressing thoughts 116
house cleaning 77, 88
House of the Lord 62, 88, 89
hug My Children 118
Humble Little Child 99
humility 8, 23, 46, 55, 65, 75, 87, 98
hungry heart 112
hurting 28, 36
I am excited 113
I am in control 13, 43, 44, 102, 103, 114, 118
I will be you 84, 85
idols 13, 68, 117
imitate Christ 65
immaculate . . 9,25,45,47,54, 59, 64, 65, 75, 80, 84, 108,
125, 126
Immaculate Conception 64, 65
Immaculate Heart . . . 25, 45, 47, 54, 59, 64, 75, 84, 108,
125, 126
implement the teachings 78, 84, 89, 107, 110
impurity 65, 87
indescribable 26
indwelling . . 60,72,75,76, 78, 81-84, 86, 89, 93, 96, 110,
116
indwelt 35
infiltrate 61
infinitely joyful 92
inflamed in love 102
inform My People 103
innermost 69
innocent 18, 105
insult 73
insult to God 73
interfering 123
interior stress 115
invisible 66, 82

invoke the help *121, 122*
island *61*
island of love *61*
it is her Heart *125*
It is on-going *115*
Jesus your Lord *1, 63, 72*
job *50, 83*
joined to Hell *99*
joy . . *13, 15, 19, 21, 23-26, 28-30, 32, 33, 36-38, 40, 41,*
44-46, 49, 51, 53, 57, 58, 62, 63, 68, 70-72,
77-80, 82, 85, 93, 94-96, 99, 101-103, 108,
110, 111, 113-115, 117, 119, 120, 121-123,
129-131
joy of Christ *62, 63, 68*
joyful . . *33, 52, 74, 92, 100, 101, 104, 109, 112, 115, 116*
just a summary *76*
Key chain *93*
kill your own will *80*
kind *21, 59, 65, 75, 124, 126*
kind and gentle *75*
kingdom . . *1, 3, 5, 10, 23, 24, 29, 40, 45, 46, 48, 63, 68,*
70-72, 79, 80, 82, 86, 89, 94, 95, 100, 101,
103, 108-110, 116, 118, 122, 124, 127, 128,
130-132, 134
Kingdom coming *10, 100, 131, 132*
Kingdom of the Divine Will . . *45, 82, 101, 110, 130, 131*
Lady of Virtues *65*
lamb *40*
large family *132*
laziness *61*
learning *14, 17, 29, 33, 59, 66, 81, 83, 84*
lesson *58, 98*
let go *13*
let His Will reign *42, 77, 107, 108, 125*
life is freshness *115*
life is vitality *115*

life of new creation *103, 104*

light . . *15, 18, 27, 28, 30, 31, 48, 55, 65, 66, 70, 79, 80,*
84, 97, 100, 104, 107, 119, 127, 132

light will shine *104*

lights *55, 84, 88*

limit *86*

limit them *86*

lion from a tiger *99*

little brother *91*

little flower *57*

little infant *98*

live in the clouds *112*

live suspended *119*

live the teachings . . *40, 51, 56, 83, 90, 91, 101, 105, 111*

locked *58, 92, 93*

locksmith *93*

loneliness *136*

lost in peace *102*

love *1, 7-10, 13-137*

Love is It *95*

love is the cure *105*

Love is union *94*

love of Christ *62-64, 124*

Love will triumph *1, 60, 70, 100, 103, 104*

Love will win *60, 70, 126*

love without end *123, 125*

love without measure *40, 123, 126*

love your Mother *89, 94*

loving the Trinity *30, 108*

lust *24, 65*

magic formula *68*

maintain this perspective *113*

maintaining *30, 53*

many astray *111*

mark on your forehead *87*

mass *44, 46, 69, 75*

maze 13, 19, 64, 123
measure 19, 22, 25, 26, 40, 56, 123, 126, 132
meek with no anger 75
meekness 40, 63
meekness of Christ 63
messenger of hope 102, 103, 122
minute 22, 23, 27, 32, 53, 55, 115, 123
mismanagement 61
mission . . . 13,19-21,24,26,29,32, 34, 41, 42, 46-49, 51,
                54, 55, 58, 68, 70, 71, 82-84, 91, 95, 101,
                103, 109-112, 115, 117, 120, 121, 122, 124,
                127-129, 132
molding you 98
mom . 8, 33, 34, 39, 40, 42, 48, 49, 51, 90, 94, 117, 122,
                130
moment . . 10,17,19,20,22, 25-27, 30, 32, 35, 37, 38, 41,
                42, 44, 45, 49-52, 57, 58, 60, 62, 68, 69,
                73, 74, 77-79, 81, 85, 87, 90, 91, 92, 94,
                102, 103, 107-114, 117, 122, 123, 127, 129,
                131
mommy . 8, 32, 42, 59-61, 66, 70, 74, 76, 79-82, 84, 88,
                89, 91, 93, 101, 105, 107, 111, 125, 128,
                129
monetary system 88
money 62, 73, 90, 98
mortification 76
mortify your thoughts 87
most precious gift 43, 130
mother 1,8,14,23,25, 26, 28-32, 39-41, 45-48, 50-53,
                55, 57, 58, 61, 63-66, 69, 70, 72-74, 76, 77,
                79-84, 87, 89, 91, 93, 94, 96, 100, 102-106,
                109, 110, 113, 116-119, 121-130, 132, 136,
                137
Mother of your dreams 74
motivation enough 80
mountain 18, 60, 61, 63, 73, 79

mountain lake *79*
mowing the yard *85*
must be reborn *93*
must have hope *1, 106, 117*
My Apostle *84, 85, 102, 104, 108*
My Arms   *14, 15, 21, 22, 27, 29, 57, 78, 80, 93, 96, 121,*
123, 137
My Bouquet *72*
My Brothers *25*
My Calmness *46, 120*
My Coming *15*
My Directive *1, 72*
My Family *16, 24, 43, 48, 71*
My Father's Wrath *87*
My Flower *1, 72*
My Gift *63, 136*
My Hands *22, 45, 62, 103*
My Heart   *1, 9, 18, 23, 24, 29, 31, 32, 34, 45, 52, 53, 57,*
59, 60, 63, 64, 69, 70, 72-74, 78, 81, 84-87,
95, 96, 99-101, 104, 106, 107, 108-111,
113, 114, 116-119, 122, 123, 126, 128, 132,
135
My Light *55*
My Love . . *1, 10, 13-15, 18, 19, 22-27, 44, 45, 50, 53-55,*
58, 66, 70, 72, 73, 77, 78, 82, 85, 90, 95,
96, 103, 104, 108, 109, 113, 114, 117, 119,
121, 132, 135, 136
My Mother . *1, 14, 29, 40, 41, 46-48, 50, 52, 53, 57, 61,*
64, 72, 73, 76, 77, 79, 81, 82, 84, 87, 91,
93, 96, 103, 104, 109, 110, 113, 117-119,
122, 123, 125, 126, 130, 136
My Mother's Army *104*
My Mother's Heart . . *1,47,52,53, 72, 77, 84, 87, 96, 103,*
109, 110, 113, 118, 123, 125, 126
My Orders *71*
My Passion *136*

My Peace *13, 23, 24, 44-46, 52, 53, 66, 107, 120*
My Plan *88, 114*
My Saints in Heaven *126*
My Serenity *46*
My Smile *28*
My Soldier *15, 50, 57, 71, 84, 85, 90, 104*
My Spirit . . *9, 30, 45, 51, 52, 54, 72, 84, 88, 91, 95, 96,*
104, 114, 115, 118, 120, 123, 138
My Will . . *1, 9, 10, 13-16, 19, 20, 22, 24, 25, 30, 35-37,*
41, 43-50, 52-58, 62, 70, 72, 73, 78, 85, 86,
88, 90, 91, 94, 96, 97, 98-100, 102-104,
107-111, 114, 117, 121, 123, 132

near midnight *67*
negativity *115*
neighbor *14, 31, 35, 37, 42, 63, 67, 74, 77, 79*
never deceive anyone *99*
new Earth *101, 107, 120*
new era . . . *1,7,9,16,25,31,33-35, 37, 41, 44, 49, 58, 61,*
65, 72, 73, 88, 100, 101, 107, 108, 114
no cares *58, 91*
no fear *17, 26, 45, 103, 111, 128, 135*
nothing . . *1, 8, 18, 26-28, 35, 36, 40, 45, 46, 52, 53, 55,*
56, 66, 71, 72, 73-76, 78, 82, 84, 85, 89,
90, 94, 96, 101, 102, 104, 110, 111, 113,
115, 122, 126

nothing is impossible *74*
nothingness *90*
number one *85, 92*
nurture love *92*
oak tree *85*
obey *122*
objects of use *65, 114*
ocean of evil *61*
Omnipotent Will *73, 78, 81*
one body united *131*
One Flock *88*

One Shepherd *48, 88*
optimum results *83*
Our Evangelist *93*
Our Light *27, 70*
overwhelmed *109*
own . . . *1,13,14,17,22, 30, 31, 35, 42, 43, 49, 54-56, 58,*
64, 68, 72, 76, 77, 80-82, 85, 86, 89, 93,
98, 102, 105, 106, 109, 110, 112, 113, 115,
119, 120, 122, 124-126, 129, 130
pace *21, 83, 97*
pack *64*
paradise . . *25, 34, 48, 49, 60, 66, 73, 114, 120, 131, 132*
passing *15, 16, 19, 51, 67, 70, 72*
past *17, 30, 44, 45, 47, 50, 67, 76, 77, 80, 88, 122*
patient *51*
paying bills *98*
peace . . *8, 10, 13-15, 17-28, 30, 31, 33-41, 43-46, 48-55,*
57, 58, 60, 62-66, 68-70, 73-75, 77-85, 88,
90, 91, 93-96, 98, 100, 101, 102, 103,
107-123, 127, 129-131, 135, 136
peace of Christ *62, 63*
peace of heart *107*
perfect *18,24,27-29,32,43, 46-48, 59, 71, 72, 76, 77,*
81, 89, 95, 96, 110, 117, 119, 123, 125,
129, 130
perfect image *24, 96*
perfect the teachings *96, 130*
perfected *44, 50*
perfection *21, 78, 107*
perseverance *91, 97, 122*
personally *27, 128*
perspective *16, 113*
physical *33, 36, 37, 77*
physical preparedness *77*
pilgrim *68*
pilgrimage *79, 121*

place of stars *107*
plan of salvation *48, 117*
plane *19, 20, 51, 63*
planned *13, 21, 68, 71, 81, 85, 101*
plant seeds *38, 65*
plateau *63*
pleasure oriented *67*
positive *61, 118*
possess *31, 52, 72*
possessed *18, 51, 54, 69, 95, 96*
pot *61, 108*
power plant *96*
powerful . . . *1, 48, 60, 64, 68, 72, 78, 82, 109, 110, 114,*
116, 121, 128
powerful Archangel *121*
powerful position *128*
praise . . . *48,54,66,68,69,78, 82, 86, 107, 111, 115, 116,*
121, 124
prayer . . . *7,9,24,25,27, 38, 42, 51, 64, 67, 75, 82, 106,*
111, 116, 135
prayer warrior *111*
precious *38, 43, 65, 79, 93, 109, 118, 125, 128-130*
presents *130*
pride *14, 65, 77, 97-99, 101, 105, 112, 124-126*
priests *7, 76, 109*
priorities straight *113*
priority *29, 64, 75*
priority of your life *75*
problems *18, 19, 29, 51, 105*
productive *43, 61, 92*
progress *51, 66, 101*
promise *7, 57*
prophet *102*
protected *37, 41, 45, 58, 87, 103, 105, 111, 116*
protection *59, 77, 98, 111, 117, 121, 122, 127, 128*
protective barrier *67*

provide *25, 38, 49, 62, 82, 90, 95, 98, 99, 123*

providence . . *20,22,24,25,36, 38, 40, 42, 44, 72, 77, 88, 102, 103, 106, 117*

publish the book *70*

pure . . . *13,20,34,39, 55, 57, 59, 65, 67, 73, 80, 81, 84, 95, 99, 103, 105, 109, 115, 122, 124, 126, 130*

pure ecstasy *130*

purest love *93*

qualities *37, 40, 55, 78, 84, 85, 115*

quality *55, 61, 63*

Queen of Peace *63, 64*

Queen of the Angels *122*

Queen of the Divine Will *127, 128*

raft *61*

rags of worry *118*

raised on love *105*

raised up *66*

reach *27, 44, 50, 99*

realize the power *61, 109, 110*

red roses *68*

redemption *10, 65*

redwood trees *64*

refine *66, 78*

refined diamond *103*

reflection *18, 54, 55, 66, 83, 92*

refreshed *71*

reign *1, 9, 19, 24, 31, 32, 34, 35, 37, 42-46, 48, 49, 54-56, 58, 59, 61, 65, 69-72, 75-78, 80-82, 84-88, 92, 100, 102, 106, 107, 108, 109, 112, 115, 116, 120, 122-126, 129-131*

reign forever *130, 131*

reinforce them *106*

rejection *47*

relax *22, 117, 130*

remnant flock *78, 87*

renewed Earth *108*
restful *71*
retirement for all eternity *96*
return to the homeland *112*
rich *117, 132*
rock of hope *116*
rooms you can walk in *90*
rosary *28, 136*
rose *16, 60, 72*
rotten heart *92*
rough edges *66*
rule *16,33,42,43,54,56,60, 61, 65, 71, 78, 86, 88,*
107, 118
rule with an iron rod *118*
rut of sin *69*
rut of vice *120*
saint *68*
saints *53, 83, 86, 102, 126*
same credit *83*
sanctity *27, 69, 132*
Satan *23, 33, 48, 65, 67, 88, 103*
Satan will be chained *33, 88, 103*
saved until now *114*
scheduling *110*
Scripture *48, 111*
sea of love and peace *116*
sea of the flesh *64*
secure *14, 36, 37, 53, 57, 62, 93, 128*
securely locked doors *93*
seeds *33, 38, 64, 65, 85*
self interest last *120*
selfish *32, 34, 67, 68, 131*
selfishness *27, 61, 101*
sense *46*
serene state *92*
serious *1, 72*

servant *56*

Serve others *22, 23, 126*

shade *95*

share . . . *1,28,40,55,60,95, 100, 102, 104, 107, 109, 124*

sheer awe *72*

shelf in My Heart *1, 72*

shell *67*

shelter *38, 98*

shine *13, 28, 46, 55, 60, 64-66, 76, 84, 92, 104, 109*

shining *79, 84, 90, 92*

shoreline *14, 17, 27, 61*

short segments *78*

signs of the times *67*

simple *15, 68, 122, 129*

simplicity *14*

sinner's hearts *93*

slave *7, 13, 14, 87, 90*

slavery will end *108*

snowflake *63*

so shocking *116*

soar *79*

social structure *88*

soft clay *57, 67*

soldier *15, 25, 38, 50, 57, 71, 84, 85, 90, 104, 110*

solvent *67*

souls . . . *9,21,23,25,27,28,33-35, 38, 43, 46, 50, 51, 55,*
56, 61, 64, 67-69, 75, 76, 78, 79, 82, 84,
88, 90, 91, 95, 100, 109, 110-112, 119-121,
136

source *33-35, 39, 59, 71*

spark of love *84*

speak the truth *99*

speck of dust *75*

spirit and life *78, 103, 104*

spirit of love *52, 92, 95, 97, 103, 104, 124*

spiritual *7,8,33,36-38,51,66,77, 79, 80, 82, 107, 111*

spiritual Mommy *107*
spoke the truth *99*
spread the good news *131, 132*
spread the words *1, 72, 101, 132*
spring *34*
sprout *33, 63, 64, 67*
stable *17, 37, 52, 95, 97*
stars *97, 107*
start anew *113, 123*
start your adventure *103*
state of disarray *116*
stay in prayer *106*
stay on track *117*
step *38, 50, 98, 123*
storm . . . *15, 17, 22, 27, 32, 34, 41, 61, 73, 81, 87, 104,*
106, 108, 114, 116, 120
storm must come *120*
straight 'A' student *95, 96*
strength *26, 28, 30, 35, 39, 61, 71, 95, 108*
strengthened *37*
stretch you out *97, 99*
striving . . . *13,16,18,26,27,41,43,48, 50, 76, 77, 80, 83,*
85, 94, 120, 122, 127
strong and robust *31, 76*
strong foundation *81*
study *16, 29, 45, 46, 59, 61, 71, 76, 122*
suffer *67, 81, 136*
Suns of lights *84*
supernatural *115*
surface *49, 59, 78, 88, 104*
surrender *15, 24, 25, 30, 42, 44, 56, 62, 83, 135*
sweet fragrance *72*
swept away *104, 106*
swim *22, 53, 78, 107*
teacher *66, 96*
teaching . . . *15,16,19,23,26,30-32, 35, 41, 45, 48, 49, 51,*

60, 66, 77, 80, 81, 97-99, 106, 120, 128

terrible mixture *123*
test *53*
the disasters *116*
the key is *80, 81*
the lost sheep *119*
they have hope *113*
they will not recover *110*
This is the plan *117*
thought life *86, 87*
thought of sin *40*
thoughts *17,20,25,28,44, 45, 50, 53, 58, 62, 71, 72,*
                78, 86, 87, 89, 90, 101, 102, 106, 109, 116,
                                        118, 123, 125
throne *39, 86, 88*
time . . . *1,7,9,13-15, 20, 21, 24, 27, 28, 32, 36, 37, 39,*
                42-44, 47, 49, 50, 54, 56, 59, 61, 66, 67,
                71, 72, 76, 77, 81, 82, 87, 90, 94, 97, 107,
                108, 110-112, 115, 116, 120, 121, 123, 127,
                                        128, 130, 135

time is running out *120*
tomorrow *21, 29, 69, 73, 81, 89, 100*
too large to count *132*
too many happenings *122*
torch *32, 104, 122*
totally reborn *132*
totally renewed *132*
totally transformed *95, 132*
towering heights *95*
transformation *24, 54, 67, 70, 80, 96, 108, 115*
transparent *28, 35*
traveling to Hell *119*
treading water *19, 22*
treasure house *59, 72, 73, 94*
treat *18, 68*
tree of life *95*

trial *16, 33, 34, 60, 106, 116*

trim *66*

Trinity *17,19,21,23,25-30,39,40, 49, 52, 53, 55, 58,*
59, 63, 65, 73, 74, 77, 78, 82, 88, 95, 97,
101, 103-105, 107-111, 115, 119, 121, 127,
129, 132

triumph *1,7,8,27,54,60, 64, 65, 70, 78, 84, 94, 95,*
100, 103, 104, 113, 125, 126, 134

Triumph of Love *7, 8, 70, 84, 94, 95, 104, 113, 134*

troubled *25, 30, 39, 73, 77, 101, 102, 107, 136*

true Christian *72*

true church *20, 31, 73, 111*

trust . . . *8,14,19,22,23, 25-27, 39, 40, 42, 51-53, 56, 61,*
62, 70, 73, 76, 77, 88, 91, 93, 98, 102-106,
109, 110, 114, 117, 118, 121, 122, 129

trust in My Love *19, 70, 73, 77, 114, 117, 118, 121*

trust not in men *88*

trust totally in God *106*

trusting in money *73*

trusts in Daddy *105*

truth *10, 13, 15, 20, 34, 65, 70, 99, 100, 102, 126*

turn into honey *73*

turned upside down *25, 68*

ultimate goal *16, 42, 113, 130*

ultimate prize *79*

unceasing *28, 44, 46, 100*

unconditionally *1, 100, 115*

unite *20, 64, 67, 82, 83, 105, 109, 111, 121, 136*

unlocks the doors *93*

unrest *17, 38, 65*

unselfish *80*

unselfishly *59, 115*

upset *23, 30, 40, 41, 92, 101*

upstream *22*

use these keys *92, 93*

vanish . . . . *54 vanquish* *61*

vanquished *104*

vast ocean *49*

very powerful resource *110*

victorious *60, 70*

vision of the calm *114*

vision of the future *106*

vocation *14, 38, 46, 52, 75, 94*

void of life *114*

void of love *114*

void of pride *124, 125*

walking flame *96*

walking Jesus *71*

walking with your Angels *109*

wasted *14*

weak *44, 113, 136*

whisper *118*

white gown *118*

wife *38, 107*

wild beast *86*

window *27, 54, 68*

window of your will *68*

winning souls *67, 68*

winning team *41, 78*

without error *127*

witness *48, 70, 115*

wonder of it all *112*

wonderment *10, 72, 101, 129*

Word is God *102*

words are special *128*

words of love *101, 113, 126, 128*

work . . *1,18,28,32, 34, 36, 38-40, 44, 47, 51-53, 64, 74,*
80, 81, 83, 89, 90, 94, 106, 107, 118, 122,
123, 129, 137

world is dying *92*

world would self-destruct *113*

worries *22, 53, 54, 85, 102*
Worry is anxiety *97*
worrying *77*
worship *25, 66, 77, 100, 107, 109, 121*
wreath of peace *63*
yesterday *113*
You are engaging *122*
you are weak *113*
you will be protected *87, 116*
you will fly *79*
you would melt *73*
your Father *18, 30, 48, 77*
your homeland awaits you *107*
zero *72, 90*